MOBILE HOME

ASSOCIATION
OF WRITERS &
WRITING PROGRAMS
AWARD FOR
CREATIVE
NONFICTION

A MEMOIR

For Heidemarie,
thanks for all your support of
my work - it means so much!
I hope you travel well in
these pages!
My best,
Megan
8/29/2020

HOME

IN ESSAYS

MEGAN HARLAN

THE UNIVERSITY
OF GEORGIA PRESS
ATHENS

Published by the University of Georgia Press
Athens, Georgia 30602
www.ugapress.org
© 2020 by Megan Harlan
All rights reserved
Designed by Kaelin Chappell Broaddus
Set in 10/14 Bodoni Twelve ITC by Kaelin Chappell Broaddus

Most University of Georgia Press titles are
available from popular e-book vendors.

Printed digitally

Library of Congress Cataloging-in-Publication Data

Names: Harlan, Megan, author.
Title: Mobile home : a memoir in essays / Megan Harlan.
Description: Athens : The University of Georgia Press, 2020. |
    Series: Association of writers & writing programs award
    for creative nonfiction | Includes bibliographical references.
Identifiers: LCCN 2020007543 | ISBN 9780820357928 (paperback) |
    ISBN 9780820357935 (ebook)
Subjects: LCSH: Harlan, Megan–Homes and haunts. | Authors,
    American–21st century–Biography.
Classification: LCC PS3608.A7438 Z46 2020 | DDC 811/.6 [B]–dc23
LC record available at https://lccn.loc.gov/2020007543

FOR MY FAMILY
AND OTHER
NOMADS

CONTENTS

ACKNOWLEDGMENTS

I'd like to acknowledge that these essays were originally published in the following literary journals:

AGNI: "Spider Season"
Arts & Letters: "Mobile Home"
The Cincinnati Review: "Several Londons, 1977"
Colorado Review: "A History of Nomadism"
Hotel Amerika: "Likelers"
The Smart Set: "Setting Stonehenge"
Superstition Review: "Motel Childhood"
Under the Sun: "What Is Vanishing"

I am deeply grateful to the literary magazine editors who published these essays and edited them so beautifully, especially Sven Birkerts, Jennifer Alise Drew, and Bill Pierce; Stephanie G'Schwind; Kristen Iversen and Lisa Ampleman; David Lazar; the editors of *Under the Sun*, as headed by Heidemarie Weidner; Patricia Colleen Murphy; and Melinda Lewis. My great thanks to Robert Atwan for citing "Spider Season" and "Mobile Home" among the "Notable Essays and Literary Nonfiction" of the year in *Best American Essays* (2018 and 2019 editions, respectively): it is thrilling to be recognized in an anthology I read and admire every year. Many heartfelt thanks to Joni Tevis, who selected "Mobile Home" as winner of the Susan Atefat Prize for Creative Nonfiction, and to Laura Newbern, Peter Selgin, and the *Arts & Letters* editors: that great honor helped me envision the collection as a *book*. Enormous thanks to Ronald Spatz, editor of *Alaska Quarterly Review*, who accepted (via a memorably rare from-Alaska phone call one Sunday morning) a tricky early essay I wrote about my father: that publication inspired so much. I'm eternally grateful to Debra Monroe for selecting this manuscript for the AWP Prize in Creative Nonfiction: it's a seismic honor and beyond-words meaningful to me. It's been my privilege and a true pleasure to work with the team at the University of Georgia Press, including Walter Biggins, Jon Davies, David Des Jardines, Thomas Roche, Sarah C. Smith, and Beth Snead; my great thanks for all their fine, insightful work as they brought this book into the world. So many wonderful and thoughtful people have supported and helped shape this book, but I could not have written it without the candor, memory dives, and excellent sense of humor of my mother, Sherry Harlan—whose wit, caring, and generosity inspire me every day. Love and special thanks to my brother, Evan Harlan, a talented architect and huge-hearted person, for talking architecture with me—and always nudging me in the right direction. Finally, all my love and gratitude to Liam, my brilliant, kind, and joyful fort-builder, and to Matthew Culligan, always my first reader (really listener), who makes everything he brings his mind and heart to more fun, joyous, and alive.

MOBILE HOME

A HISTORY OF NOMADISM

It is not down in any map;
true places never are.
—HERMAN MELVILLE,
Moby-Dick

1. Black Tent

In the deserts near my home in Dhahran, Saudi Arabia, Bedouins pitched their black tents. This was the late 1970s, but the
same style tent once housed Abraham and Moses, according
to the Old Testament, and pre-dates those books by millennia.
Out in the sands, I'd scan the horizon for the tents' low-slung
pentagram shapes, for the camels and cooking fires. My dad
told me Bedouins are the most gracious of peoples, that hospi-
tality is the cornerstone of nomadism. He said desert nomads
will starve to give a visitor—even a visiting enemy—a meal. This
was what interested him: insights into the varied social universes intrinsic to his career managing international contracts.
But it was the black tents that repeated in my seven- and eight-
year-old mind like a favorite song.

Their stark premise exhilarated me, then as now: a primary residence that is portable. The tent-home is as intimate and nimble as room-sized clothing. It untethers the domestic world from address, lightens it to a freedom of movement. Its inhabitants must plant roots someplace other than a patch of earth, a hometown's fixed proximities, instead reaching ambient, skyward. Maybe a nomadic child grows like an epiphyte, all nutrients critical for development absorbed from the traveled-through atmospheres—fabrics of light, language, scent, and sound, their inherited and intuited meanings.

2. Synaptic

I have a history of nomadism. Growing up, I moved on average once a year, lived in seventeen homes across four continents—very particular corners of North America, Asia, Europe, and South America—by the time I graduated from high school at age seventeen. Like traditional pastoral nomads, my sense of home was as temporary as a campsite. But unlike them, my family's "campsites," our homes, were never revisited. No seasonal structure directed my family's movements; no terrain was deemed ours—our family's, our ancestors'—to revolve around with grazing animals, whether goats or camels or sheep; no regular orbit of travel arranged the world into a geographic pattern my family might call, on the grandest scale, a home.

Yet nomads we were, twentieth-century people from the developed world moving far and wide to "develop" the rest of it. What directed our travel were my father's white-collar jobs on massive engineering and building projects—the very construction that halts traditional ways of living, spreads postmodern clockworks, technologies, transit systems. The culture we brought miniaturized weeks of overland travel into five-hour

flights and fused intricate synaptic cross-stitchings of city-
scapes, histories, cuisines, topographies, religions, artworks,
and languages—all as we'd found them in our own constantly
shifting backyard.

My family's version of nomadism continues an original
American tradition: to chase that setting sun. Going back
just as far as "America," nearly all my ancestors were typical
colonial-era religious refugees who had to get out of the Old
Country in a hurry. Three to four hundred years ago, these
people boarded wooden ships from Atlantic Europe to North
America and landed in a history lesson of the colonies—Plym-
outh, New Amsterdam, Massachusetts Bay Colony, Philadelphia, and dozens more. Then their descendants surged
through one frontier after another, inexorably west, until all my
great-grandparents were born west of the Mississippi; all my
grandparents raised their kids in Washington, Oregon, or California. And my parents, not to be stymied by the continent's
Pacific coastline, leaped up like a sneaker wave and landed in
Saudi Arabia.

Why did my parents do this? For the money, yes, but probably not any more money than had they stayed put. Their hun-
ger for distance—and thus mine—seems inborn, intractable.
My mother quotes her Tigris, Missouri-born father on his own
family's restlessness: "We are called to the next mountain."

What are we trying to find there? What do we create from
mobility, from the drive that transfuses the imagination and
reroutes the intellect into maps we can't help but follow?

3. Box

My parents drifted over my brother and me like mostly sunny,
sometimes unpredictable weather systems able to cyclone us

suddenly around the planet—to the streets of Lahore, Rome, Cairo, Dublin, Panama City, and Bangkok; of Kathmandu, Edinburgh, Bogotá, Heidelberg, Jubail, Amsterdam, and Nairobi; of Hong Kong, Athens, Mombasa, Kuwait City, Frankfurt, London, and Abu Dhabi.

So like any nomadic child, I learned to apprehend places differently than settled people do. During all the travel, as each of my homes was replaced by another, again, another, again, those seventeen times, the world loosened for me into flexible components: the view from another kitchen window, shadows cast by unfamiliar trees, my self refracted through more strangers in a new classroom. Patchwork, scraps, jumble—these fragments pieced into a perspective that lacked a solid middle distance; that place we take for granted to be "real life" kept disappearing on me. Over time, only the very near (inside my head) or the very vast ("London," "astronomy," "poetry") felt tangible or trustworthy or discoverable. This ongoing abstraction was abetted by cardboard.

Because we lived mostly out of boxes. Boxes in various stages of being packed and unpacked, sealed up, sliced open; carted off to a moving van or storage; sitting in my new, strange-smelling bedroom. Boxes always ordered or rustled up by my mother, kept track of on yellow pads in voluminous detail by my mother, packed and unpacked with extraordinary speed and skill by my mother. My mother was a homemaker, both in the "did not work outside the home" sense and, far more concretely, as she settled and dismantled our multitude of homes. Meanwhile, my father was nearly always "at work"—that phrase a partial cover for his secret, deepening absence, one that would earn him the label "extremely high-functioning." He, by contrast, rarely did any packing.

4. Architect

Bedouins call themselves *Ahl al-Bayt*, or "people of the tent."
Their tribes once numbered in the hundreds, though all are
said to share an ancient and highly reasonable bias against sedentary townspeople for being—in comparison to them—slow,
soft, and materialistic. The word *Arab* itself has roots in nomadism; in ancient Hebrew, the term was often used to describe
tent-dwelling desert people, just as Muhammad used the term
in the Quran centuries later. Bedouins trace their patrilineal
ancestry all the way through Ishmael, son of Abraham, back to
Adam. But only they live as Ishmael once did, in tents woven of
hair from the black goats led from place to place for grazing,
along routes followed since a continuously relevant antiquity.

The weaving of the tent fabric is done, not so surprisingly,
by women. Women also design the tents. They fabricate them
by hand, expand them as their families grow, replace pieces
as they wear out. And it is women who pitch the tents. Women
construct and settle the campsites—tasks usually accomplished
in less than an hour. When it's time to go, they dismantle and
pack up the tents and belongings in equally brief time.

Women have performed this form of home-building in
every black-tent tribe—whether Bedouin or Berber, Kurdish or
Tibetan. And they've done so in nearly every other traditional
tent-dwelling culture across Asia, Europe, and North Africa:
like the Tuaregs, who weave animal skins into their goat-hair
tents, or the indigenous peoples of Siberia and Lapland, whose
conical, wool-and-animal-skin tents—like the Sami *kata*—are
primarily fabricated by and always pitched by women. In North
America the iconic tepees of nomadic Plains tribes were owned,
designed, and constructed at each campsite by women.

The word *architect* contains this lightly buried cultural leg-
acy. It derives from two Greek roots: *archi*, director, and *tec-*

tos, weaving. To be an architect once meant to conceive and create a moveable housing of textiles or sewn skins—dwellings lightweight enough to be transported on a camel or donkey or horse yet strong enough to withstand the elements. And among nearly all traditional tent-dwelling peoples, the idea was synonymous with being female.

5. Print

Paper, as for any book lover, manifests *journey* for me: the horizon-like sweep of page, print's ink trails leading the reader onward. But the moving boxes' paper is ingeniously built for literal journeys, origamied into usefulness of the most practical kind: cardboard strong enough to hold almost anything.

Like covers to unwieldy books, each box was scrawled with a title that doubled as setting: LIVING ROOM, EVAN'S ROOM, KITCHEN, BATHROOM. Sometimes subheadings followed: "Neal's papers," "Sherry's sewing machine," "Sherry's books." Most boxes featured the word *books*—my mother's family value. Though we would never settle into a permanent home, we would always have enough books, shipped around the planet at considerable expense. Books mimic adrenaline to the narratively restless: nests of worlds in which the mind takes predestined flights from time and place.

The boxes were numbered 1-89 or 1-112 or 1-136, like too many chapters in a rambling, episodic novel. Together, they told a story, attempted a plot that defied any classical arc, featuring exactly no suspense, climax, or development. The characters they depicted—American family of mom and dad, daughter and son—were merely owners of some items that kept moving around, without explanation, cause, or effect. Boxes got packed, unpacked, shuffled from home to home, storage unit to moving van to shipping container in an obsessive, nonlinear ritual. One box perpetually belonged in a well-stocked, country-style kitchen. One contained certain "Sports Equipment." Another box, "Spode fine bone," was stashed in our Houston two-car garage, then vanished from a truck heading west.

6. Storage

My mother grew up in houses filled with boxes, as her family moved to college towns up and down the West Coast for her father's teaching and coaching jobs. These moves performed for her how "home" was never there for long, so how much did it really matter? Boxes enabled my brilliant father's escape out of tiny Big Bear, California, away from his "broken" childhood home, and toward a world where his wits could take him—almost literally—anywhere. It's as if he thought, *Anyone can have a home, but not everyone can travel the world the way we can.*

"When we get all our boxes out of storage . . ." opened my family's favorite fairy tale. But our boxes never stayed out of storage for long. They protected our belongings, while also preventing them from being swept into the drenching continuum of life, the coherence—however messy—of a family home. The boxes were strong enough to compartmentalize even that.

They still do. Today, nearly all my parents' possessions are housed in boxes in my mother's storage unit in Seattle.

7. Belonging

Traditional camel-herding Bedouins live with the sparsest essential belongings. Even their tents are minimalist compared to hardier nomadic structures like the yurt or tepee, which possess heavy freestanding frameworks constructed of wood or wattle. By contrast, a black tent may be pitched using a single pole, the fabric stretched into shape by a tensile network of long ropes, hooked from the fabric panels and pegged deep into the ground. The poles, fabric, rope, and pegs together compose the framework, each element interdependent in holding the structure in place. This is a mobile architecture so ingeniously sturdy yet lightweight that it's been in use since the Stone Age.

Most nomadic tents consist of a single room divided into distinct zones of living. In Bedouin black tents, women and children sleep in a larger space on the left side, with men's sleeping rolls confined to the right. A fabric flap divides the two sides, and it's lowered when male visitors are greeted on the men's side—also where the coffeepot resides. But nothing, including social convention, prevents women from joining in any conversation. Bedouin women may not be seen by male visitors, but they can very much be heard.

Bedouins traditionally make nearly every item they own, their caravan a self-sustaining transit system of food and shelter. Goat-wool yarn is hand-spun by girls as they walk; freestanding looms are kept near the open cooking fire, where women weave the fabric for their family's clothing, bedding, and domicile; men sit outside to work the camel-skin leather saddles they use to ride their camels. Sleeping usually takes place inside the tent, but Bedouins prefer to live outdoors. They consider the desert, its vastness and desiccation and horizon, to be their true home.

8. Terrain

The entire world—or at least where the most lucrative engineering projects might be occurring—opened up to my family as a potential future home. At one point, India was mentioned. At another, Indonesia. An unsettling discussion involving a transfer to Connecticut occurred. My family didn't move to these places, but their shapes, their possible breaths, bumped against my own history, my immediate future, parallel universes that might suddenly rope around my present, palpitating self.

Meanwhile, on the ground, my feet rattled across another new hometown I'd come to know intimately. No one expected me to like it. I was expected to grasp it, get by in it, and I did. I learned to suss out everything meaningful I would ever feel about a place within about twenty seconds. It flashed inside me like a nuclear cloud, a revelation of the collective habits we call culture, the sensory gauze of terrain.

When people ask where I'm from, my answer is always in some way a lie, not that I mean it to be. I don't know where I'm from, but who wants to hear that? The answer should be easy, should help supply a label, though I've always been struck by how geography seems the least questioned destiny. You can't really know what your world determines about you: where it ends and you begin. It would require a map of all the places and times you said no to it, where and when you said yes, and how deeply you meant it.

9. Room

The sky never leaves you—a fact so stunningly obvious it's easy not to notice the experience of it. But when you live on the move, on the road, the sky's presence magnifies, can solidify into something like your room, hung and framed with directional intimacies. In this way, its expanse opens your vision onto other, more proximal senses, like your sense of freedom, of exposure, of safety.

The sky offers a special promise to the nomad: that freedom is safety.

As a child, I decide there is nowhere I cannot handle with this gleaming room above me—one that, as I move around the world, collapses lower or vaults wider, shines a blue opaqued with gray or heat-distilled yellow, bristles or brightens or mists against my skin. But that it's always the same place is a refuge.

This begins in the Arabian desert, where whatever in me—in any of us—that vibrates to the night sky's indigos and fizzing tides of constellations learned to reach out in soul-like volumes to join with it, then rest beside it, as at a campfire.

The night sky inspires a genre in the Bedouin oral tradition called stellar poetry. Lyricism merges with logistics in its language, since desert nomads discern their lifetimes of journey from the constellations, which unfurl ever-changing maps of time and travel to the wettest places. Orion moving south with the months, rainfall during Pleiades or Ursa Major. These and other celestial signals tell the Bedouins when to get a move on. In his book *Arabia of the Bedouins*, Dutch diplomat Marcel Kurpershoek describes living with Bedouin tribes in the late 1980s and early 1990s so he could collect their poetry—none of which had ever been written down. "We have the clumsy term 'oral poetry' for this phenomenon," Kurpershoek observes. "The Saudis simply call it 'rhyme, invention, chant' or 'words.'" When Canopus returns, it sits low on the southern horizon, described in tribal verse as "red and beating like a wolf's heart."

10. Children

Most of us in the settled West know the Bedouins' world—if we do at all—from the writings of such adventurers as T. E.

Lawrence, Wilfred Thesiger, and Isabelle Eberhardt. I grew up around Lawrence's and Thesiger's books and discovered Eberhardt's just before traveling to the Sahara Desert in my twenties.

In *Seven Pillars of Wisdom*, T. E. Lawrence, or Lawrence of Arabia, describes visiting a ruin with Syrian Bedouin: "We went into the main lodging, to the gaping window sockets of its eastern face, and there drank with open mouths of the effortless, empty, eddyless wind of the desert, throbbing past. . . . 'This,' they told me, 'is the best: it has no taste.'"

Wilfred Thesiger, the English explorer and travel writer who first mapped the Rub al-Khali, Saudi Arabia's Empty Quarter, wrote in *Arabian Sands*: "In the desert I had found a freedom unattainable in civilisation; a life unhampered by possessions, since everything that was not a necessity was an encumbrance."

Born in Geneva in 1877, Isabelle Eberhardt moved at age twenty to Algeria's Sahara Desert—where she lived as a Bedouin man, converted to Islam, married an Algerian soldier, and wrote prolifically until her death in a flash flood at twenty-seven. In *The Oblivion Seekers*, she wrote: "But the vagrant owns the whole vast earth that ends only at the nonexistent horizon, and his empire is an intangible one, for his domination and enjoyment of it are things of the spirit."

Especially in contrast to the overstuffed, busily furnished West, no solitude is more buoyant, saturating, or crystalline than an open desert's. But unlike these European-born writers, traditional nomads—like the very Bedouins whom these writers befriended and admired—are never escape artists, loners, vagrants, or iconoclastic adventurers. Or anything close.

Nothing kills the mood like a screaming baby, but the fact is, nomadism is based on family life. Bedouins by definition live with their nuclear family and extended tribe in tight, temporary quarters that move with their herds, the colloquial "fields on the hoof." Yet this central narrative of nomadism—the one in which the children are raised—is mostly omitted or diminished in their books.

In my own nomadic family, my parents viewed their children as the world that mattered most, and as long as we were all together, our location was mere detail. But "our family" was an ideology that sometimes lacked practical application, as if belief in its absolute good absolved any breaks in logic or common sense. *Would moving our children three times in one school year and twice the next be detrimental in some way to their development?* was not a question either of my parents asked. After all, we could take the kaleidoscopic beauties and riches and wonders of our travels with us anywhere. They could assemble around us like a fanciful wardrobe, invisible yet dramatic as the emperor's clothes.

II. Chatwin

Bruce Chatwin goes deeper. In *The Songlines*, he weaves a quasi-fictionalized travel narrative about the Australian outback into a gorgeously speculative theory on nomadism and the origins of human language. He describes the "songlines" of the nomadic Australian Aborigines, a genre from a culture dating back forty thousand years, as songs that map out the continent by landmark and associated ancestral mythology, from one line or node to the next, as sung by someone walking at a four-mile-per-hour gait. Language and movement through place thus cohere like an auditory map—and help prevent the singer from ever getting lost.

But this journey into lyrical ethnography is interrupted by Chatwin's thoughts—raw, vital, searching thoughts—on his failed ten-year project: a book on nomadism. This section of

The Songlines is called "The Notebooks," a globe-wandering composite memoir of Chatwin's travels with nomads. One of its anecdotes stands out for me, involving a tent-dwelling Bedouin sheikh in Mauritania. The sheikh answers Chatwin's question about why he continues to live in the Sahara with all its hardships, why it is "irresistible" to him.

This is the sheikh's reply: "Bah! I'd like nothing better than to live in a house in town. Here in the desert you can't keep clean. You can't take a shower! It's the women who make us live in the desert. They say the desert brings health and happiness, to them and to the children."

As a woman, a mother, I'm fascinated that it is the women who—if Chatwin and that Mauritanian sheikh are telling the truth here—love the freedom of nomadic living more. Is this because, in so many societies, the settled life is harder on women, restricting their movements into a stifling domestic sphere? And perhaps no one can see that more clearly—can see it, indeed, *at all*—than a nomadic mother grown used to the shifting horizon as her family's terrain. She may be responsible for tending the fire, but that fire is always on the move.

This ancient way of life appealed to my mother: all the arrivals in new homes she'd soon leave behind. She didn't seem very interested in living in these homes, at least not for long. It was in their making and unmaking that she excelled, as if the homes themselves comprised an extreme, materially creative form of travel.

12. Dream House

As a girl, I often constructed my dream bedroom in my head. It usually overlooked a Swiss Alps lake. Beside the tall white bed, fireplace, books, and cats, flokatis featured prominently.

I was alone there, hidden away as long as I wanted to be.

But—I'm squinting my eyes here at the memory of myself as a girl imagining myself in that room—I was also not moving much.

I was safe but motionless, in perfect suspension. Living never entered into it.

"Thus the dream house must possess every virtue. However spacious, it must also be a cottage, a dove-cote, a nest, a chrysalis. Intimacy needs the heart of a nest." This is French philosopher Gaston Bachelard, from his ravishing treatise on domestic metaphysics, *The Poetics of Space*, in which he examines the classic château of a bourgeois Frenchperson's childhood as a setting for phenomenology. He transforms rooms, major pieces of furniture, and personal effects—an attic, a cupboard, a collection of seashells—into philosophical and psychological archetypes of language and identity.

Bachelard does not address freedom of mobility in relation to this dream house. Freedom is not a component beyond one crucial activity: the ability to daydream there. He's transfixed by the settled person's dilemma: how to extract from a singular home a universe's meaning?

The nomad has different issues, an exact inversion: how to sculpt from rootlessness an identifiable, meaningful universe? Or, put more unnervingly, how do we attach meaning to constant change?

Even as a child, I understood we can't attach anything to change and that this can form a spiritual directive. During our travels, my father grew interested in Buddhism, started meditating twice daily, a practice he kept up for decades. He taught me how early on, and I've toyed with meditation ever since. It has beauty—like the sensation of pure, bright safety. But like my dream bedroom overlooking that alpine lake, it's a retreat into stillness, the body left eerily motionless.

13. Privacy

In one of his books on human geography, *Space and Place*, Yi-Fu Tuan makes this distinction: "Place is security, space is freedom; we are attached to the one and long for the other."

Those contrasting definitions of space and place are exceptionally useful. But since nomads of whatever iteration are attached to space and its freedoms, how secure do we ever feel in a single place? I long to feel at home anywhere, without also getting squirrelly with claustrophobia over nothing more constricting than a normal house that is purportedly my own. It pins me down; they know where to find me. Mobility, by contrast, brings the supplest, most inventive of privacies.

Was this one reason my parents adored the rush of travel, the flexibility of never committing to any place? What they didn't do was commit to these untethered, unbroken parts of themselves. They didn't say: *We are nomads; there is no getting around it.* They kept pretending they could make permanent homes. They couldn't. And their many failed attempts to settle down—to slow themselves into the sedentary—finally hollowed into vacancy, into loss.

My parents viewed address as an easily remedied accident, chased locational adventures like they were game, wielded an unshakable curiosity in this world's many forms, thought best on their feet. What they couldn't do was stop, and stay healthy.

This is what a nomad is. What I am.

14. Looking Glass

In 1866 an eighteen-year-old Civil War veteran, after walking for two months with the Fisk Expedition—a thousand-mile trek from Saint Cloud, Minnesota, to Montana's then-rumored gold country—wrote to his mother: "I am in good health and am enjoying myself to the best of my abilities. I have not been sick a day or hour with the exception of sore feet. Some of the party are discouraged, homesick, and consequently in the worst of humors, cursing the country, the Expedition, etc. I am glad it is not in my nature to get discouraged easily or to look on the dark side of every picture. We have six weeks yet to travel before we reach our destination. I can see the Missouri and Yellowstone Rivers from the door of my tent."

This teenager was my great-great-grandfather, Wilson Barber Harlan, and the door to that tent—the green and blue rivers it opens onto—is one I've imagined into a made-up memory. My father read me this letter when I was a kid, from an article written by his uncle for the *Journal of the West*. It created an inspiring legend of my family's true nature.

Over the next decade, W. B. Harlan and other Montana settlers claimed lands long considered home by the Nez Perce people, who'd lived as nomads along the region's rivers for centuries. W. B. Harlan cultivated the lush valley along the Bitterroot River with the vast apple orchards that would make him wealthy.

In July 1877 the Nez Perce leader Looking Glass passed through the Bitterroot with his tribe, fleeing U.S. Army soldiers sent to force them to live on a small reservation in Idaho. W. B. Harlan and other local men were tasked with stopping them— but they let the tribe pass unscathed. Criticized for this pacifism, Harlan defended it in the local paper, writing, "When we overtook the Indians, Looking Glass . . . told us he would not harm any persons or property in the valley if allowed to pass in peace, and that we could pass through his camp to our homes. . . . We were not silly enough to uselessly incite the Indians to devastate our valley."

Looking Glass and his tribe would suffer heavy casualties a few weeks later, during the Battle of the Big Hole, and by October the Nez Perce would surrender to confinement on the Idaho reservation.

15. Proxy

Great cities are proxies for nomadism. Cities are where most nomads—if only by nature—live these days.

I moved to Manhattan at twenty-one, walked for the next nine years whenever I could, walked to avoid the subway, walked to avoid the cost of a cab, walked because I love to, round and round and round that island. New York City was spacious enough, varied enough, shot through with thousands of miles of layered, coiling pathways. Stand still and everything around you changes. Its vastness mimicked, for me, the open desert's—just crazily compressed. Instead of every star or color of heat, the sky is filled with people; windows; electricity; gossip; clanging, moving slices of architecture. In these multiplicities of closest proximity, you can wander, Escher around the place, for as long and as far as you want. And so I did, until I recovered from my dad's death from alcoholism and wondered where else on earth I could live.

I wanted "home"—so I went back to California, where I'd lived on and off, off and on, since infancy. But California, where I am today, doesn't feel like my home. It is home for my son and my husband. And that, for now, is enough for me.

16. Stagecraft

Six months after having our son, my husband and I moved into the only house we've ever owned. This home is the "more" I wanted for my son that I, growing up, never had.

It is not a metaphor. It is not an emotion or a sense of family.

And home is not where the heart is—that cliché bearing all the catchy idiocy of propaganda. If you don't have a home, you can still have a heart. You can still love and be loved. Your heart might be in any number of places, with any number of people.

Home is an actual place. It is a location. It has a roof. It can generally be expected to be there when you get back, filled with your stuff.

A home is simply and vastly the backstage of life. It makes private the grinding literality of daily needs: bed, food, bathroom, wardrobe. It doesn't have to be pretty, but it does have to make sense to you. Too much drama backstage—will it be there? why have the stairs moved? who are all these new people?—sucks energy from your performance under the lights. You are left feeling restless, literally unable to fully rest, to recuperate anywhere. That can force you out onto the stage, into constant, free-form performance. Adults can often handle this, even enjoy it, embrace the adrenaline. But children need to learn how to belong somewhere or they may never figure it out.

I know this because if it weren't for my son, I would still be rootless.

17. Scale

A racket starts, distant at first, like metal scraping metal. It plays up and down my nerves, atonal and grasping. The more I try to breathe it away, soothe it with cultural surrogates—concert, restaurant, museum, yoga class, play, more books—the more it scratches from inside my skin.

At a certain point I need to go wandering. My feet need to hit earth, again and again, that bone-filling drumbeat. I need the sky's colored threads to tangle inside me, pull me somewhere new.

Just the smell of cardboard boxes—book, dust, intoxicating anonymity—still flexes my deepest pleasures and fears: of drift and disappearance, secrets of far and more, all the world ready to melt inward and sensory. I often fend off these desires like an addict, since I never want them to stop. I struggle to keep them in proportion, to a sedentary scale.

Like the sound of the boxes' cardboard flaps scraping against each other, enough tension to hold together, to fight us off a little. The scrape and sweep and nick of the packing tape, whistling off its roll, sealing the boxes closed.

Then we get to slice the boxes open in the new place. Stacked in a garage, a storage unit, they wait for the next move, to anywhere at all. They are sturdy yet flexible, until they are used one too many times, begin to bend like heavy fabric, the outer fiberboard peeling off the corrugation, revealing a design composed largely of air.

SPIDER SEASON

> It is not enough to conquer;
> one must learn to seduce.
>
> —VOLTAIRE,
> *La Mérope française*

1. Venom

I don't feel the bite, only the poison—a rare hemotoxin that kills red blood cells. I never see the spider, just my outer left thigh swelling like a water balloon. It sears with heat, a darkening scarlet. I find my way to the ground. My hands cup the growth as if to keep it from bursting while my attention snaps: it's still *me*, this thing.

My dad carries me to the car, drives my family to the emergency room, where a doctor administers a steroid shot, a painkiller, then lances the mound. Out drains heavy yellow liquid threaded with blood—the most gut-turning bodily substance I've seen. Who knew so much gunk could be in there? *There* being me.

"Probably a brown recluse bite," the doctor tells us. Lots

of brown recluse spiders in this part of Texas, he continues. One of the deadliest spiders in North America, along with the black widow—a creature known for its aggressive ways—but the brown recluse almost never attacks. You'd practically have to roll in a nest of them to get one to bite you, he says.

My bad luck amazes the doctor for its sheer unlikelihood; he seems excited and impressed. It's an anecdote he will probably tell: how this nine-year-old girl managed to get bitten by a brown recluse spider in the manicured suburbs of The Woodlands, Texas, while walking with her family one Sunday afternoon. They'd stayed on the path. Nobody saw a web. Who knows how the shyest of spiders got to her?

The doctor sews several stitches and sends me home. The experience marks my first trip to the ER, and it is a harbinger of sorts. The next year, I'll catch what appears to be a stomach bug in the Colombian jungle village where my family is living and be flown to Bogotá, where I'm treated for a near-fatal case of typhoid. I'll have a life where strange incidents catapult themselves, via invisible leverages, into otherwise average days.

Of course, unlucky events regularly visit us—in sneak attacks, in showy bombardments—though probably not in any pattern we can discern, and no doubt some of us more than others. We're noodling along in our usual way and a poison finds us, and only us.

For a year after the brown recluse bite, every time I see a spider, I scream as if on fire. I scream as if the monster has already chewed off my arm. I scream at the fear I didn't know pooled inside me. The poison infects me with my one lifelong phobia. I will say my fear is of spiders, but even as a kid, I knew the fear was not so precise, so confined. A phobia turns a natural occurrence into a highly personalized form of black magic. And it's one that will shapeshift over time.

2. Porch

Hard-driving creaturely skittering sure as a leg-propelled bullet. Pins-and-needles-down-the-scalp incarnate. Appendages proportional to madness: eight legs akimbo as living hair, stretching high-pitched from a stump of head. Eyes by the pair, fours, half-dozen, scattered across the midriff, or none at all. Poison-injected needlepoint fangs mistakable for yet more legs. The unexpected strike.

Now it's my son who is nine. Fall, where I live in California, marks spider season, when all species of spiders seem to take over the land. No need to decorate our front porch for Halloween: it will already be lashed with webs propagated by brown garden spiders lurking by the dozens above our heads, around the light in gauzy high wires. Instead of grabbing brooms, my family grants them pet names: the oversized Itsy Bitsies, my son's all-purpose Spidery, my attempts to teach him mythology with Arachne and Spider Woman and Anansi.

Where did my arachnophobia go? It ate new, related realms when I had my son. Now my phobia's black magic requires an adult-styled sacrifice: an exact inversion of my instinctive response. Now I must stay put, breathe away the thrums of panic, study the spiders' movements, and never, ever kill them. On a practical level, this is the only viable alternative I've found to my fear of eight-legged creatures, to screaming and running away from them, to providing regular, startling bouts of slapstick comedy to family, friends, and random passersby whenever I happen across one.

In payment and over time, my emotional equipoise will vanquish other sources of fear, other traumas lurking out of view. This belief constitutes magical thinking, I know. And it's in full swing just in time for Halloween, when I've also let the spiders' finespun dwellings collect inside my house, as the air chills, and I am most in the mood to be at home.

That "home" sounds so easy, ordinary, but for me it's been a loaded, dangling, impossible state of place. I now live in my first real home, created when I became a parent, after dozens of moves, dozens of worlds that kept getting swept away, some-times—as if by reflex—by my own hand.

3. Myth

Arachne, I tell my son, is a young woman from Greek myth famous for her beautiful weavings. I go with Ovid's version: how Arachne starts bragging that she's a better weaver than her teacher, Athena, who tracks Arachne to her village and demands a show of humility for the girl's goddess-given talent. Arachne refuses, and the two compete in a weaving contest. To Athena's surprise, Zeus judges Arachne's tapestries the win-ner—even though they depict the Greek deities getting up to no good. Furious over Arachne's genius and hubris, Athena trans-forms her into a spider: cursed in form, but still able to weave so the world can enjoy her skill.

Anansi in African-rooted folktales is a spider who weaves patterns of words that can outwit, charm, or bamboozle anyone. In a popular tale, Anansi befriends an old man who inconve-niently turns out to be Brother Death in a peckish state. Death follows Anansi home, chases him and his family up a tree, then waits for them to tire and fall into his mouth. From that height, Anansi spins some tempting blarney, convincing Death that spiders taste more delicious fried in flour. When Death drags over a bag, Anansi jumps into it, blinding Death with a spray of flour so his family can escape.

And in the native religions of many Pueblo tribes, Spider Woman, or Spider Grandmother, is a great creator who thought the universe into existence as a whole and interconnected web. In one Navajo creation myth, she acts as both trickster and savior, stealing a water monster's baby so he will flood the subterranean realm, thus forcing the first humans to seek safety above ground. To help them ascend to this world, Spider Woman also weaves these original people a raft and a ladder, and later she teaches them to make their own patterned webs using a loom.

In all three of these world-wandering, millennia-old tales, the web, more than the spider, is the focal point. Whether it symbolizes artistry or intelligence or creation itself, each narrative web illustrates our human need for larger patterns of meaning—for discerning the existence of these patterns and our ability to manipulate them.

And I can't help but notice how, in these stories, the spider's venom, potential danger, and creepy-crawliness are forgotten. This must be why: outside our own species, only spiders produce in visible, concrete form anything approaching the complex structures—the multidimensional, fibrous, semicrystalline geometries—that animate, compose, and tripwire the human mind.

We may not like spiders, but we cannot get enough of their webs.

4. **Strength**

Every time we're on the subject of spiders, my son informs me that spiderwebs are the strongest substance in the world. The reason they're so strong is because they are dense yet bendable, he tells me. An inch-thick diameter of spider silk could stop a jet mid-flight, while a similarly sized piece of steel would snap, as demonstrated once in an educational cartoon he used to watch.

That creatures so small could make *the strongest thing ever* thrills him. It is thrilling to the small-boned and less muscular among us: that strength lies in nothing so obvious as a mean right hook but in materials particular to our natures that coalesce into what we can produce and—the real trick—maintain. How tensile are our creations? How clever and adaptable their design? How quickly can we restart, re-envision what gets destroyed—so much will—and get back to work?

And: How to create a structure strong enough to sustain us and our families over the longest possible span of time? This is the unremarkable and all-consuming responsibility of parents. For nine years, I have taken the need for this structure very philosophically, very metaphorically, and very literally.

I grew up with an idea of home so shiftless, melodramatic, and globe-trotting it rarely possessed a recognizable framework: a chaos so rich and saturating it taught me to see patterns in the unlikeliest of places. But I will not replicate that with my son. What looks like average good fortune—the ability to provide a single comfortable home, neighborhood, and school for him—requires heavy effort and vigilance for people like me: the children of the emotionally itinerant, of alcoholics and other volatile off-in-their-own-worlders. Patterns of normal can feel like anything but to us.

Spiders secrete domicile, spinning new webs as often as each day. My parents set up and dismantled homes with a similar quick-witted motility—the substrate of time guiding their constructions even more than the setting, seeking out job assignments of one year, or three months that stretched to six, or two years cut down to ten months. Threaded in between were our half-dozen interstitial quasi-homes: the winter in a fancy London hotel, the two highly weird weeks spent in a Kuwait City sublet because of a logistics snafu.

Like nomads anywhere, my parents traveled with their favorite weavings: the silk-and-wool carpets bought in Isfahan; the Bedouin rugs, blankets, and pillows haggled over in the souks near our homes in Saudi Arabia's Eastern Province in the 1970s. Out in the desert, Bedouin families were still living in black tents, following nomadic traditions going back more than ten thousand years. Given the million or so years of hominid hunting and gathering before that, you could argue that some form of nomadism—of living on the hoof, via improvisational homemaking—is what humans are built for.

In practice, in the modern world, and without any prey, livestock, or seasonal grazing to shape our migration patterns—to slow us down to a particular vantage of stars and atmospheres, of topography and tribe—my family's white-collar nomadism left scattershot marks. As a kid, I learned to be good at making friends and also that I never got to keep any. Though born in Vermont, I often feel like an immigrant who can never fully adapt—only without an original home to yearn for. But this has given me flexibility, the reflex to look, perhaps, in more directions to find and build sustenance.

5. Octagon

Spiderwebs are not eight sided, but that is how I've always drawn them, how my son does, how it's easiest: draw an axis of two perpendicular lines, overlap a second axis at a forty-five-degree angle, then connect this framework with swooping lines. The spider's eight legs must be where this idea comes from, web as curvy, symmetrical octagon, as a signal of warning, a stop sign.

Octagons are shapes I've viewed with delight ever since traveling as a child in the Muslim Middle East, where geometry forms the basis of all visual arts and intricate patterns fill in where the human form is absent (the latter for religious reasons). There, octagons regularly give spatial orientation to towers, mosques, and atriums, and tile work often depicts kaleidoscopic linkings of octagons. The shape makes me think of a faceted compass rose, the eight cardinal directions planed around an inner sanctum.

The Crusaders brought the octagon-as-design-element to new corners of Europe, and a couple of centuries later, Leonardo da Vinci became obsessed with the shape. As an apprentice sculptor, he worked on the iconic octagonal dome of Florence's cathedral, Santa Maria del Fiore. Later, in his notebooks, he drew octagons into nearly every architectural plan, experimenting with the unique ways it contains both circle and square. Then there is his famous Vitruvian Man: a young man's body spread-eagled inside the circumference of that circle and square, using two superimposed versions of the figure to form a spider-like, eight-limbed person with four arms, four legs. Noting paired elements such as how the length of the man's arms matches his height, da Vinci believed sacred architecture should reproduce the mathematically related measurements of the male human body—and, to the point, Jesus's own form.

6. Habitat

Orb weaver spiders use their bodies to measure their webs, determine the length and strength of its strands. They choose from among seven or eight types of silk to spin, each composed of different chemicals and nanocrystals. Orb weaver webs most resemble the swooping octagons of my drawings but are, in reality, irregular; eight-sided shapes are extremely uncommon in nature. These webs feature any number of radii thrusting from a central hub, spiraling frame lines anchored to whatever substrate the spider is working with: porch walls, plant branches, patio chairs. The webs are never symmetrical, never adhere to the common human delusion of perfection, of predictability and its safeties. The breaks in each web's pattern do not form a pattern because spiders know how to adapt their work to the ever-changing world.

We make a home to establish a baseline of safety, to force a pattern of predictability around us. Often we do it—as the saying goes—for the kids. My son loves our neighborhood filled with friends, our garden's hodgepodge of drought-friendly plants he's careful to keep an eye on, his easy walk to school, the parks where he's graduated through all the age-based play structures, the Berkeley grocery stores where he sources his idiosyncratic treats: raw honey sticks, organic chocolate malt balls. He never wants to move from our house, he tells me; he admires how the prism hanging from our front window sprays rainbows around the living room, how his snug bedroom is "so big"—roomy enough, it is true, for his books and toys, a desk for drawing, and for any requisite blanket fort-building. The kitchen always feels bright to him.

This is the child's-eye view of home I always yearned for: making sense of the world by collapsing its boundaries to a single set of family-scaled proportions. Security is a temporary state of being, but it's capable, with some work and much good fortune, of being captured in the physical and emotional ecosystem of a home.

So I watch and marvel at my son growing firmly in place: it's the first time I've seen anyone do this, never mind my own child, never mind in the home I helped make for him, and so too for myself.

7. Luck

Having lunch in the backyard during an Indian summer day that has billowed, global-warmly, into November, my son, his friend, and I spy a quarter-sized, brilliant orange spider hanging from gleaming bridge lines between rose stems. A white butterfly flutters toward it. "Fly away, butterfly!" we advise. We are eating apple slices, and none of us gets up to wave it off. A few minutes later, the butterfly's tissue-fine wing catches in the web, and the spider darts in to wrap it. I feel some guilt as all three of us jump up to watch. "Cool!" my son and his friend say in unison.

I've never seen a spider the color of saffron—a vibrancy that reminds me of the robes worn by Buddhist monks in Thailand, where I've traveled many times since childhood. In that country's Theravada tradition, all creatures in the universe are interconnected and sacred, so killing of spiders and bugs is a no-no. They deserve their lives as much as we do.

Across European cultures, it's considered unlucky to kill spiders, a superstition that makes practical sense in a way few others do: the spider eats pests like flies and mosquitoes, creatures that produce nothing—from the human perspective—but trouble. But magnanimity or practicality are not the reasons I save every spider in my house. Either I save it or I ignore it until my husband arrives. When he grabs the spider with a bunched-up wad of paper towel, I plead with him, "Don't kill it! Don't kill it!'" as if our own lives depended on it. I can't kill them because I have to save my family from doom. Yes, I understand how stupid that sentence is. When it comes to spiders, all the dark arts get wrapped into one package for me.

We ascribe luck or misfortune to natural phenomena or, a little more gracefully, see everything as happening for a reason: the will of a deity, fate, or "the universe." However it happens, it's a relief—at least for me—to temporarily externalize my own fears of Sudden Bad Things onto harmless, nonsensical targets. Superstition cannily employs the exact randomness we fear could take us down.

8. Evolution

I consider spiders to be "grotesque," "disgusting," and "nasty," but of course they embody nature at its most natural; these so-called horrors are built into the system. The ripping and shredding and scrambling and stinging—it's as organic as clouds or milk, fur or feather. Or, for that matter, the silks and gauzes of spiderwebs: as a species, spiders have been spinning webs for more than one hundred million years, totaling a number of webs so large, it whispers toward the limitless. As for the creatures themselves, all we can hope to do is avoid contact or numb ourselves to them, or shove them offstage if we can.

Or—like my son—you can love spiders. You can be the first kid on the field trip to the wildlife reserve to hold the live tarantula in your hands, beam a smile as it crawls—in high-stepping, fuzzy-limbed slow-motion—up your left arm. You can delight in learning that native tarantulas scurry around the hiking trails of a nearby mountain, nest in underground dens they blanket with webbing, are considered about as docile and dangerous to humans as kittens. You can find them fascinating and beautiful for the exact characteristics—the prominent row of spiked teeth, the fangs that bend at powerful joints—that terrify your mother.

There I stood with the group of chaperones, not screaming, forcing breaths as I tried not to imagine the tarantula strangling my son's face, only to envision this scenario like a prophecy. Afterwards I told him over and over how proud of him I was.

"But why?" he asked in all seriousness. "It wasn't scary. Don't you want to hold one?"

I don't remember my answer—probably many "no's" hitched to nervous laughter. But of course he'd ask me this. All he knows is that, in our home, I protect spiders and tell stories about them, point out their clever webs. He must have sensed what I, under my phobic curse, could not: that his mother, too, loves spiders.

MOTEL CHILDHOOD

> Like lost children we live our
> unfinished adventures.
>
> —GUY DEBORD,
> *The Society of the Spectacle*

1. Cars

When you are six, you move into a motel in Los Angeles with
your mom and your little brother. For six weeks you live on
the second putty-colored floor, behind one front door and one
front window overlooking a Denny's and a shear wall of freeway.
Palm trees droop over asphalt, the native garden of parking—
cars that come and go in ever-shifting colors and patterns. Your
mother doesn't have a car anymore. You came and will leave
here by taxi.

2. Diner

It is the bicentennial year, and every day can look like the
Fourth of July. Denny's flickers with miniature American flags

planted along the walls and booths. This is where you eat every meal during your stay at the motel.

At breakfast the waitress with the frosted blond upsweep greets your family, asks about you and your brother. She talks about her kids, older now. She knows you should be in school but aren't. She always lets you pick the same booth. She brings your mother all the coffee she can drink.

Every morning, you get silver dollar pancakes you smear with butter and pile with powdered sugar, a dense snow-cover that yellows with butter, grows crunchy as the pancakes cool. These pancakes are the most delicious things you've ever tasted. As the weeks go by, you don't even order them: the waitress just brings them right over, with little paper containers of powdered sugar dotting your plate.

Your brother sits next to you. He is half your age, about half your size, and you worry over him like he is a squirrelly blond pet. He likes syrup more than powdered sugar on his silver dollar pancakes, which strikes you as absurd. But you know this is the high point of his day, and yours, and so you stop forcing him to eat powdered sugar and let him get syrup all over himself.

The Denny's morning-shift waitress is the only person outside your family you talk to most days.

3. Space

The first place that slammed the words *motor vehicle* into *hotel* is up the coast in San Luis Obispo. It dates to the 1920s, when cars first hit California like an amphetamine to the nervous system. Your motel was built in the Space Age—the era when chain motels constellated along American interstates by the tens of thousands—and its modernist veneer is showing signs of wear.

Like a space station, it provides only the barest necessities for human survival in its environment, for people bending time and space in new ways with their travel. What's new: you can drive anywhere, faster than people have ever traveled by land; you can always stay the night in a motel.

Your dad grew up in Big Bear, a ski town high in the San Bernardino Mountains, a range you can see on clear days from Los Angeles. As a teenager in the 1950s, your dad, with his two brothers, tinkered under the hood of one beautiful but broken-down car after another. Your father's pet car project: a rusted-out Austin-Healey, which he nursed back to glory during college in L.A. and sold before he married your mother, a sale he will speak of as one of the biggest regrets of his life.

Your mom lived all over the West Coast growing up, including towns very close to your motel—Pasadena, Monrovia, Altadena. Your mother still talks about how, when she was young, her father loved to put her and her mom in the car on the weekends and just drive: pick a road and see where it goes. These were some of the happiest times of your mother's childhood— driving fast with her family, with no destination.

But your family has no car at this motel. Your family spends almost all day in the room, the heavy front curtain pulled over the natural light, which your mother says is important for privacy. Shadows cover you like sheets of water, soaking the usual motel room features in grays and dark blues: two beds, a bathroom with a bath, a nightstand with a Bible in the drawer. A dresser your family fills with nothing. A television your mother never turns on. Carpeting she warns you is filthy, no matter how much it's vacuumed.

Your family is set to move to Iran. Your dad is in London until that happens. Iran, to you, might as well be in outer space. London might as well be the moon, since it does seem closer, and you have heard of it, in books. You'd never heard of Iran until your parents began discussing it as your next home. You will get there by flying to London first.

But then, one week at the motel, Iran changes to Saudi Arabia. You will move there instead because Saudi Arabia has lots of oil and America is having an oil crisis. Americans need oil for gasoline so they can drive around their country as fast as their cars will go. It's a big country. It's fun to drive fast. It's fun to be free to drive anywhere you want; you can always stay the night in a motel.

Your mother is not happy about staying in the motel until a taxi will take all of you to LAX. Then you will travel to London, and then Saudi Arabia, and then dozens of destinations that will seem chosen as if from random stops on a spinning globe— Kathmandu and Mombasa and Abu Dhabi, Hong Kong and Heidelberg and Athens, on and on and on. No one knows when you can leave, when you can start all of this. Your mother hates to wait, she is always saying. All these years later, you wonder who on earth likes it.

4. Witness

In the motel room, your mother collapses like a star. Whatever she is feeling billows inward, stifles into the state of waiting. What this looks like is a lot of motion that results in nothing, or almost nothing, or nothing visible. Pacing, unpacking, repacking, reshuffling items, activities that revolve around and around and wind up very close to where they started. The enormous force within your mother re-implodes by the hour, scaling downward to a figure seated in a dark room or walking around it. Often she is reading by the nightstand light. Usually you are reading by the nightstand light. Your brother is playing on the filthy carpeted floor with his toy cars.

Outside, cars shoot across the freeway so fast you can never know anything about them. Yet you are a constant witness to the fact of them.

5. Gone

A few months ago, your mother described to you one of her earliest memories, from when she was three or four, and it's a new story to you. She and her mother were living in an apartment in Portland, Oregon, while her father was away, serving in the Navy during World War II. And her mother left the apartment late at night to visit a friend—another wife of an officer—down the hall. But your mother didn't know this. Your mother went to sleep, woke up in the dark, and found her mother gone. She panicked—wailing, yelling, knocking on walls and doors. It felt like hours that she ran around the apartment, screaming for her mother. Finally, she tired herself out and was discovered—when her mother returned home—asleep, tear streaked, on the floor.

Her mother was right down the hall, having a drink with a friend. But she might as well have been on Mars. Her mother might have been speeding down a freeway going who knows where. Disappearance is solid in those moments. It is a loss that glazes and fractures all the space around it.

Some places beckon for these kinds of disappearances or present them as a dare: all the motel room doors lined up along a hall, an outdoor walkway. These places seem disposable, built for throwaway nights. You could choose this door, or that, or one on the first floor. You could step inside it and disappear forever, take on another life, leave in a different car. The randomness tantalizes, broken from any weight of self. It's like the game of pretend when toddlers close their eyes and think they're hidden from the people around them, except the game is turned on its head: it's you who might pretend to disappear from your self, into a new world that could hide you from it, through places you can't yet imagine.

6. Doors

Your mother chooses another door: a book cover. These doors could lead anywhere. You have many small doors in your bag. The motel room is paused while you enter them, line after line like path after path, street after street. The spaces inside them billow wholeness, planed and enfolded with direction.

You cannot build a home out of a dozen small doors in your suitcase. But you try.

You pass through one into a place near Oz, where trees grow magic lunch pails. You sit on the bouldery rocks, as the shrieking Wheelers—human-like creatures on all fours, with wheels for feet—retreat. The sandwiches in the magical, sprouting lunch pails remake themselves over and over for you: thick-cut white bread with ham and butter. You snap off the little glass bottles of milk. The sun on your face, the metal lunch pail hot to the touch, you take out the cloth napkin, the apple, the slice of cake. After lunch, you will join the others—Dorothy and the talking hen, also from Kansas—as they find a locked door carved right into the stone hills. They have already discovered the key. Their travels seem both random and lucky: the best kind.

The Oz books, like this one—*Ozma of Oz*—were some your mother's favorite books, too, as a kid. They are the rarest of classic fairy tales: American. They were dreamed up by a traveling salesman.

You re-emerge into darkness, the motel room. All these years later, you still enter those shadows, with books, the twilight that disappears now into wherever you can imagine. It's a home, or familiar as one. Because as much as you've tried, you don't remember leaving the motel.

SEVERAL LONDONS, 1977

> The one duty we owe
> to history is to rewrite it.
>
> —OSCAR WILDE,
> *Intentions*

1. Tunnels

In January 1977 I move from Los Angeles to a fancy, old-fashioned London hotel suite, where I live with my mother and little brother for two months, long enough that we run out of money. We leave the city in March to move to Saudi Arabia, then return in September with my father to live for six months in a posh furnished flat overlooking Kensington Square—a private garden a few blocks from the larger, public Kensington Gardens. My family is given an iron key to the gate.

All year, London appears and disappears and reappears to me, like the world's most ambitious theater production. It turns inward, a network of tunnels always leading us deeper, backward or forward in time, color-coded streams of location in the Underground. London forms a subfloor of meanings and their breakages, my first stabs at cultural philosophy, which transpire as simple noticing.

But London starts out as thoughts voiced by my mother. My mother loves history. Like a famously cast mystery narrative, the past is alive to her, often much more so than the present—a trait I have largely absorbed.

2. Queen

London in 1977 is celebrating the queen's Silver Jubilee. It's as if the city is on fire with the queen's crowned head. Her grinning face flashes from the sides of buses, on billboards, Wedgwood dishes, platters, crown-shaped erasers, teapots and teacups, giant novelty pencils, silver lockets, tea towels, T-shirts, and key chains, and from posters in window after shop window.

My mother is not a queen person. She's not enamored of the current royal family. "Ceremonial," sniffs my mother. I too am skeptical of Buckingham Palace as we stroll past it, bundled up to our eyes against London's version of January. The palace is very big, yes, and the bear-fur-hatted guards resemble enormous toys. But what's the point of royalty with no power? The queen owns so much—the world's richest woman!—yet does so little. What kind of people would put up with this? I am echo to my mother.

In London that year, 60 percent of adults under twenty-five are unemployed. Across town a cultural revolution against the queen and all she stands for is being mounted on King's Road. But we don't know this then.

Meanwhile, the Tower of London entombs the horrible and glorious structure of royals run amok. "The little princes," my mother says, describing how their small skeletons were found under the dark stone stairs. As we wend our way around the eleven towers, she names other names—Richard III, Oliver Cromwell, Thomas More, Walter Raleigh—and recites their dooms. But it's Anne Boleyn whom I instantly adore, from my mother's tale of her bravery, her half-Frenchness, and her name, since my middle name is also Anne-spelled-with-an-*e*. "She ordered the sword that would behead her from the best sword-maker in France," says my mother. "That was smart. So it would come down in one fell swoop." For me this provides the prototypical example of the need for quality when it counts.

The original dungeon does not yet house a beautiful gift shop but is rife with dank iron racks and spiked implements that make my skin burn when I just look at them. This is how terror is intimacy.

Later I stand in the courtyard near the chopping block where many noble heads were lopped off, clutching my *Illustrated Children's Guide to the Tower of London*, getting used to the smell of the city: wet building stone, traffic fumes, the breath of people speaking their witty, snide, obtuse, brilliant, sneering, kind, idiotic, transcendent, slurring, elegant comments. I learn the world was not so friendly for grinding, crunching spans of time. The time-and-place blip of decency and ease through which my family moves appears to me, for the first time, as anomaly. *Were those Tower of London people just as human, just like anyone, me?* I wonder, watching the ravens hopping around the courtyard. *Or is that the problem?*

3. Half-Board

I'm eating roast beef in the grand restaurant with flowery carpeting and soaring ceilings and gold-framed mirrors and dozens of candlelit white-tablecloth-covered tables. It looks like the fanciest dining room on the *Titanic*. There are no other guests. It's my mother, my little brother, me, and half a dozen staffers. My mother is sneaking dinner rolls into her bag.

It's February, and the three of us are still waiting to move to Saudi Arabia. Our visas are taking forever, and my mother has run out of traveler's checks. Worse still, she has no way to reach my father, who is already in Dhahran, our soon-to-be home. This is 1977: you can't just call Saudi Arabia from a hotel lobby. Fortunately, our suite—which is paid for by my father's employer, apparently on an ongoing basis—includes breakfast and dinner in the hotel restaurants, though not lunch. This "half-board" room-and-meal configuration is a Victorian-era holdover. Every day we gorge on a full English breakfast, eat a lunch of pilfered bread rolls smeared with peanut butter from my mother's bag, and then show up for dinner right at five o'clock, when the restaurant starts service.

It's not exactly a Dickensian tale of hardship. At the time, I assume it's normal for good fortune to always be striped with weird, hard-to-explain misfortune. The young waiters have sparkly, noticing eyes and bring us extra rolls.

4. King's Road

I have no friends in London, not one, the entire time we're in residence. I'm not in school, and my mother doesn't seek out other expats or local families to find playmates for my brother and me. I am fairly isolated in a center of the world.

Diverted from kids my own age, I look outward. My extroverted nature twists toward the public, historical, epochal, aesthetic, and gossipy urban sphere, and my interior world is drawn to the street plans laid out by Roman, Saxon, and Norman invaders. I wring understanding from jewel-etched medi-

eval maps of the city and the Thames, from Renaissance mul-
lioned windows, from the swooshing-by of beetle-black cabs.

All these Londons introduce "culture" to me: a set of preex-
isting conditions of meaning allowed to reproduce instead of
many, many others. And the plot of culture is history, the story
that tells us why, say, a constitutional monarchy persists in a
parliamentary democracy.

My mother introduces me to another word: counterculture.
The more oppressive and conformist the culture, the brighter
and braver the counterculture must be. A child grasps this
instantly, as *counterculture* represents everything she wants to
do, grab, and eat but her mother won't allow.

That year, London's counterculture will be torn open by
John Lydon, aka Johnny Rotten, an Irish Catholic Londoner,
and Malcolm McLaren, a Scottish Jewish Londoner. The city
will unleash the Sex Pistols, the Clash, Siouxsie and the Ban-
shees, the Pogues, and many other bands inspired that year by
the fashions in a few storefronts on King's Road.

Later I will discern that sometimes in your childhood, you
can rewire yourself to favor or suppress your natural traits.
Sometimes it's because you don't have a choice. Sometimes
things get weird (you are living in a hotel, have no relationships
with other kids your age, etc.), and you find ways to grow anyway. From such transformative acts of will and imagination you
may never recover. In other words, you will no longer be able
to distinguish your own naturally occurring "culture" from
the seemingly opposite—"countercultural"—qualities you also
possess.

5. IRA

Just looking at the queen's omnipresent face, I'm struck by how much she resembles my grandmother, my mother's mother, née O'Malley, who, back in California, donated money to the IRA, coached me on how to correctly pronounce Sinn Féin, and told me horror stories starring Oliver Cromwell, who ordered soldiers to torture and behead Irish Catholic children, then place their heads on spikes. This happened several years back—three hundred or so. My mother tells me that this tendency is the "Irish memory," an experiential continuum where everything bad that has ever happened might as well have happened yesterday. It's a trait I recognize, having largely absorbed it.

The IRA plants bombs in London so the English will stop trying to rule Ireland, according to my mother. I hope we don't get bombed, even if it is to help Ireland. A grand department store called Selfridges was bombed and set on fire the month before.

My mother does not approve of her mother sending money to the IRA. "You know Mother," she sighs. On the other hand, she observes, "The English have no morals when it comes to Ireland."

"The Irish are pigs," sneers Margaret Thatcher during a BBC interview that year.

Yet my grandmother and Queen Elizabeth II could be sisters, they look so much alike. *How different are the English and Irish, really?* I wonder. Similar enough to want to bomb each other to bits.

6. Pants

London is hordes of businesspeople with the extravagantly vague air of spies.

London is where the world becomes visible to me, the fact that there is one, a world. I have already lived in three massive, roughhewn American states—California and Alaska and Texas—each in practice nearly countries unto themselves, places that don't care what you think of them. If the United States still assumes in the 1970s that it is what matters most in the world, then London is the first place I've been that knows all too well it *isn't*, not any longer.

London is where I first learn what an "American" is, something you can only accurately grasp after leaving the United States. A strange creature, this American. Smiling and loud, provincial but ambitious, ignorant yet shrewd, lucky and tetchy, self-satisfied enjoyer of fast food and wearer of blue jeans. I see Americans, lots of them, walking around the city, shouting their confusion about traffic laws at one another.

London teems with every nationality in the world, or so it seems to me. All these Londoners appear very long and thin. Bell-bottoms swing and make the rest of the body look like a broomstick. Skintight jeans are pegged around bony ankles. Everyone seems hungry, sharp-eyed: my first city people.

"People are sick everywhere. People are sick and fed up with this country telling them what to do," says Malcolm McLaren that year. He and Vivienne Westwood run the Sex boutique on King's Road. Along with selling blow-up dolls and shredded jeans, Malcolm McLaren has been reading Guy Debord's *The Society of the Spectacle.*

Malcolm McLaren talks about the Situationist International to anyone who will listen.

Malcolm McLaren talks about Guy Debord and the French experiment.

Malcolm McLaren admits he wants to sell a lot of pants.

Malcolm McLaren will later claim he started the Sex Pistols as a stunt. That he was the mastermind, the Machiavelli of punk.

"Everyone on the planet knows Malcolm's full of shit," says Steve Jones, guitarist of the Sex Pistols, years later.

I suspect Malcolm McLaren reads *The Society of the Spectacle* less as a warning about what we now call consumer culture—where "the commodity completes its colonization of social life"—than as a manual for exploiting it. He already envisions art and culture as broken because there is no counterculture for consumers, not really. All that is left is selling pants, the avant-garde stealing market share from the mainstream.

"Everyone is so fucking bored," says Johnny Rotten into a reporter's video camera, as he walks the streets of 1977 London, his face gleaming with gaunt twenty-one-year-old beauty—and speed.

7. Fairies

London is bunk buses, as my four-year-old brother calls double-decker buses, red and friendly looking, as if they are enchanted vehicles that can whisk you away to a magical fairy village made of tea biscuits, clotted cream, and strawberry jam. Except fairies are always clever, annoying creatures in the British Isles, like pretty mosquitoes with high IQs.

With no spending money, my mother packs the three of us off to a bookstore across from our hotel, wonderfully filled with couches, because "the English are literary," she says. We browse there for hours, buying nothing. I discover Puffin books. Over and over I read *Timothy and Two Witches*, in which a boy goes to stay with his young aunt, Melinda, who turns out to be a good witch. Her London home is alive, like a plant, sprouting tendrils that hand him a cup of milk at breakfast. Her neighbor is a bad witch. The two live in London townhouses bustling with white or black magic, sun or sleet, as divided by the property line. It will become a favorite book ever. Its London will be one of my favorite cities. I will read it to my son, who will keep it by his bed, in *his* stack of favorite books ever.

Britain makes all the best children's literature. No one has ever been able to convincingly explain why. You will hear theories involving the playgrounds of wordplay afforded by the English language or the brutality of the public school system and the attendant fondness for vivid, intuitive, and disassociated realities. Perhaps the answer involves the long tradition of those lovely, evil fairies who represent a shared sense of the real powers at play in this world and the imagination required to combat them. Of all its countercultures, England's children's literature is the most voluptuous and sly.

8. Future

On May 27, 1977, "God Save the Queen" by the Sex Pistols is released, and on June 7 Malcolm McLaren throws a party on a Thames riverboat to celebrate. Video available on the internet shows the London police arriving in speedboats to break it up. There's Richard Branson, lion maned and shirt open, who bankrolled the fete. The gathering is treated as a criminal emergency, with loudspeakers, sirens, flashing lights, and handcuffs.

American viewers might wonder: what on earth is going on here? It's hard for us to grasp that the English do not enjoy free speech in 1977. They are ruled by sedition laws, which have snared the Sex Pistols. Their particular crime involves making fun of the queen of England and having a band called the

Sex Pistols. Also, hiring a boat called the *Queen Elizabeth* and hanging a banner reading "God Save the Queen"—her portrait marred by these words in block letters—from its upper deck.

McLaren, by all accounts except his own, knew the party would be broken up in a big, flashy, newsworthy way. He wanted the Sex Pistols to get arrested. But Johnny Rotten sensed the setup, tipped off the other Pistols, and snuck off the boat. Only McLaren and minor members of the entourage got arrested.

The stunt still worked brilliantly: the words *punk* and *Sex Pistols* made international headlines. Soon, all across London, posters of the band lined walls and utility poles and telephone boxes, complete with the version of the queen's face covered in text.

In "God Save the Queen," Johnny Rotten sings for England's young, impoverished lower class—like himself; and guitarist Steve Jones, illiterate until adulthood; and Rotten's childhood friend, John Ritchie, aka Sid Vicious, raised by a heroin-addicted mother. All of them had grown up in council flats in London's outer boroughs. The song contains, among other things, an ironic manifesto about who, in 1977 London, gets a future. As their friend Chrissie Hynde—then living in London as an expat musician—later observed: "The class system is what punk was all about."

Even if Malcolm McLaren formed the Sex Pistols as a Situationist spectacle, Johnny Rotten was its scathing poet of witness. His lyrics still pierce. But Rotten and McLaren fought incessantly over the group's direction, and the singer quit the next year. Without his voice, the band dissolved, unable to signify much beyond shredded pants.

9. Fawkes

In the fall, my family returns to a London colonized by punks hanging around its street corners. We move into that flat just off Kensington Square Gardens. The park is walled off from the now punk-infiltrated public by a tall black wrought-iron fence. I'm disappointed it's just a plant garden, without a special rich children's playground for my brother and me to experience.

The flat is packed with dark old furniture and gloomy historical paintings. One portrait is of a dark-haired nobleman with greenish-pale skin, whose creepy eyes follow my brother and me everywhere in the room. The woman who owns the space rents it out furnished to families from my father's employer, who often stay for long stints in London. Is the man an ancestor of hers? An antique-market find? We do not know. But we feel like we are living in a museum of English aristocracy. I sleep in a scary dark wood bed that looks too small for average-sized adults and eat at the enormous dining table that my mother guesses is from Chaucer's day. Mainly I hang around the kitchen with the housekeeper, who works for the owner, checking in on our family and keeping the flat in fine shape.

She teaches me the opening lines to a poem:

> *Remember, remember!*
> *The fifth of November,*
> *the Gunpowder treason and plot;*
> *I know of no reason*
> *why the Gunpowder treason*
> *should ever be forgot!*
> *Guy Fawkes and his companions*
> *did the scheme contrive,*
> *to blow the King and Parliament*
> *all up alive.*

I learn about Guy Fawkes Day, but exactly wrong. It will be many years before I realize that Fawkes is burned in effigy forevermore as an *antihero*. When my family and I walk the streets of London to see the bonfires on the night of November 5, I assume they are burning him because he's a hero—a funny way to commemorate him, true, but maybe this is how they do it in England? Fawkes had wanted to blow up the English government hundreds of years earlier, which, as an American, I find reasonable. Back then, who wouldn't? The Americans, the Irish, the French—all the rebels, the idealists, and the humanists hated the English. The good people, in other words, in my child-eyed view.

10. Dickens

The next month, we go to Harrods to buy Christmas crackers, little foil tubes whose ends you pull open to reveal treats like caramels or chocolates. In the store, which is like a magical shopping castle of buyable treasures, we purchase a glass Father Christmas for our tree and Christmas pudding, nothing like packaged American pudding but instead delectable, sweet, buttery spiced crystallized fruit sauce. "London is the best place in the world for Christmas," say my parents.

This has got to be true, with one exception: Scrooge. I find myself subjected to *A Christmas Carol*, which my father has a deep love for, a love that entirely eludes me. It is a ritualized story I despise on sight. I'm not bothered that the poor are virtuous and the rich evilly selfish—that I could accept, I suppose. No, it's how the underclass take on their roles in the story like good little soldiers. Why aren't they angry? I wonder. They should be. Americans would never swallow it. Or would we?

As we walk the fairy-lit streets after seeing *A Christmas Carol* staged, my mother talks about Dickens, how he wrote stories about all the different Londons of his time, with people from all backgrounds and their funny accents. She says this was new, revolutionary: to depict a poor orphan with the same care and value, twists of fortune and black humor as a rich miser. She says London was never the same after Dickens: it became so much bigger, a city where everyone is interconnected by stories.

11. City

The next week, my mother is seized by abdominal pains and must be checked into a hospital for surgery. My father brings my brother and me to visit her in a district made of rain puddles, concrete, sloshing grayness: Lewisham. He ushers us onto the train at Victoria station, wearing his trench coat and wool tartan scarf, his face pale with worry. My brother, still slight enough to slide onto my lap, clutches his Paddington Bear like a proper English child. If we don't open our mouths, we could pass for a small clan of anxious Londoners. And this, during the last month of 1977, is what we are.

As we roll away from central London, I can't wait to see my mother. She will be fine, if groggy, in a metal hospital bed, wearing her pink nightgown in a tall Victorian room as important looking as a museum gallery. She is doted on by nurses called "sisters" who wear starched white uniforms and little veiled caps and who greet my brother and me like long-lost family.

Lewisham's London is not tourist London, not famous London: past the East End, on the South Bank, an inner borough of brick Edwardian row houses and drably modern suburban shops. But by this point, London could look like almost anything and I wouldn't be surprised.

It's a word, a sense of place I've come to love—pure as a pagan faith, an urban idolatry. I am on its side, and it on mine. At seven, I am absolutely sure London is my friend—not that it ever *told* me that.

London has taught me what a city is—and *this* I learn exactly right. A city is a place where interesting always beats beautiful. London, for all its charms, can't get by on its looks. And anyway, nature already has beauty covered. London instead contains enough tight spaces, tumult, and interested bystanders for the unlikeliest of harmonies: between architectures and texts, revolutions and royalty, exclusive parks and studded leather jackets. It layers so many histories that chronology itself seems freed, jumbling public narratives with countless private scenes, as easy to rework as taking a different street.

Visiting hours are over. My dad, my brother, and I have kissed my mother goodbye and are heading back to the city's heart. At Victoria station, we transfer to the Tube to get back to Kensington, through the now-familiar whoosh of hundreds of strangers scattering around us, the London that feels massive, yet pressed so close. I am temporarily motherless, but her voice is in my ear, the growing sense of my own history taking place, and I'm ready to take the London Underground home.

MOBILE HOME

> Would a bird build its nest
> if it did not have its instinct
> for confidence in the world?
>
> —GASTON BACHELARD,
> *The Poetics of Space*

1. Trailer

When I was a kid, my family called them trailers, and we lived in three of them: two double-wides and a single-wide. All were new models at the time, dating to various years in the 1970s and early 1980s, each clad in white metal siding, the interiors awash in the era's ubiquitous browns—wall-to-wall utility carpeting, faux wood wall paneling. Yet my childhood did not take place in any trailer parks, at least not those of stereotypical American lore.

My family's three trailer homes stood in a trifecta of extreme ecologies, as if picked at random using a wall map, a blindfold, and a few darts: Alaskan tundra, Arabian desert, South American jungle. Somewhat ironically, my family's living in these trailers, company housing in compounds, indicated our higher socioeconomic status: only white-collar employees on these massive construction projects were allowed to bring their fami-

53

lies to live with them near the sites. And no matter where these employees fell in the corporate pecking order, everyone—senior VP on down—lived in the exact same style trailer.

Though our housing compounds were constructed in the service of the most obvious, unapologetic, and transnational form of capitalism, they provided unwitting experiments in socialist housing, in the concept of residence as uniform. They removed any class stigma from the trailers themselves—laying bare for all of us who lived in them the clean, flexible utility of their designs. Whether the outdoor temperature was 125 degrees or negative 40, whether walloped by sandstorms or subarctic blizzards or tropical rainstorms, our trailers proved hardy, comfortable havens. (Granted, we never lived in tornado country.) The double-wide floor plans somehow fit three bedrooms, two full bathrooms, a U-shaped kitchen opening onto a spacious-enough living and dining area, plus numerous closets into about a thousand finely edited and functional square feet. They featured "all mod cons," as our British friends in the compounds put it: the newest kitchen appliances and state-of-the-art heating and cooling systems. Down to their metallic, mechanical core, they were literally housing "as machines for living in," to use Le Corbusier's phrase, that key manifesto of modernism in architectural design.

A mobile home is nothing new: humans as a species have built temporary shelters since our days roaming around as hunters and gatherers. But the idea of giving a house wheels, axles, and a chassis is about a hundred years old, hailing from the burgeoning American car culture of the 1920s, when automotive industry engineers first rigged up trailers in their garages for family camping trips. Since then, the mobile home has been hailed as both a promise and a curse, the adventurous future and one that has long since disappointed us, rusting in our neighbor's driveway.

And my own three trailer homes—along with the fourteen
other homes of my globe-trotting childhood—have inspired
questions I've spent years, decades, and many moves trying to answer, questions that haunt place mongrels like me:
How much do we belong to our settings? What part of home is
mobile?

2. Indiana

In coastal Jubail, Saudi Arabia, in 1978, my family moved into
the Bechtel compound that, if you squinted, resembled a trailer
park in Albuquerque. We'd just moved from Al Khobar, about
fifty miles inland, from a neighborhood of modular houses
that received good reviews from no one: on windy days, sand
infiltrated the wall seams and then misted across the rooms.
So my parents were relieved to settle into one of the sturdy,
all-American double-wides, shipped there by the Saudi royal
family, the project's client, at considerable expense.

In that scorching open desert, and without anyone telling
me I shouldn't, I adored that trailer. It *fit*, space-wise, comfort-
wise, like a correct-sized shoe. I was eight, and children tend
to intuit home as a nest, yearn for cozy rather than vast, for
the inviting, cushion-filled nooks the British call "snugs."
My mother filled our place with Persian carpets, Thai silk
wall-hangings, the small treasures of our travels—soapstone
chess set from Mombasa, a malachite egg from Afghanistan—
like we were living in the charming weekend tent of a jet-setting
sheikh. The creamy spice of Ethiopian coffee bought from open
sacks in the Jubail souk and made daily with cardamom by my
parents infused the rooms. When I came home from school, my
mom would still be sipping the stuff with her friends, women
who hailed from all over the States, Europe, West and South

Asia, North Africa, whom I ogled for their tall sandals, statement jewelry, and endless stories, since my mother seemed able to talk books, politics, food, and travel until the End of Days. For his part, my father's key addition to our abode was the stereo system big as an oven that he'd haggled for in Dhahran and that vibrated forth a part-genius, part-silly 1970s soundscape courtesy of the Kinks, Neil Diamond, the Bee Gees, ABBA, Anne Murray, Carly Simon, Elton John, Led Zeppelin, and the Muppets. So our family, our music, our small treasures constituted a unique quality within our home: whom and what we loved, lived with daily, could take with us.

But our family, our stuff: these are not, in fact, our homes.

Our home was our trailer, and the machinery of its construction fascinated me and made me feel safe. I marveled over the prefabricated pieces of my bedroom, how the lights were built into the walls and ceiling, how the doors and windows latched with the satisfying snap of a train compartment, how I was protected by a metal husk from the desert stretching just below the wheels—a house you could roll on out of there. These qualities sculpted our sense of being Other and transient in the Eastern Arabian desert, our homes imported from the distant and—to me—exotic world of Indiana.

For that was where our double-wides were manufactured: Indiana, where today 90 percent of American manufactured homes are factory built. Its middle American vernacular architecture had been plunked down, much like Dorothy's Kansas farmhouse, in a very different land.

3. Almaden

Judy Garland–as–Dorothy Gale's first step out the front door of her black-and-white farmhouse—a building sturdy enough to have survived a tornado-ride to fairy land—and into the luscious carnivalesque Technicolor of Oz remains one of the most stunning moments in film. It is pure American surrealism, its oddities brash, fetching, and candied. And its whimsical psychology tugs deep: Who wouldn't want their house to travel somewhere more exciting than its current spot amid the gray known quantities of our own personal Kansas, where grim-faced people are shoveling the pig slop of Actual Reality?

When I was three, I watched *The Wizard of Oz* on television, and it apparently blew my mind. For the next six months, I *became* Dorothy—dressing like her, only responding to her name, holding conversations with invisible witches and the wizard. But that's not all: I renamed my mother the Cowardly Lion; my father, the Tin Woodsman; and my little brother, who had just been born, the Scarecrow. After those six months of me trotting around our Almaden, California, tract house carrying a basket filled with bread and apples, referring to our patient Belgian Shepherd as Toto, and babbling about the Emerald City, my mother finally took me to a doctor. He was very interested that I could read the Oz books aloud to him, chatted with me for a while, and then pronounced me as merely being in possession of "a very active imagination." He assured my mother that my Dorothy phase would pass, which, technically, it did. I no longer carry around a basket of bread and apples, for example.

Dorothy's home flew across the sky and took her to the most beautiful, magical, and fascinating land. How this simple yet strange premise gripped and obsessed my three-year-old imagination I can't now explain. I remember flashes of donning my blue gingham apron, making the method actor's leap of faith that I was Dorothy, or that I *might as well be*. I'd moved three times in as many years, but did I register that? Had I been told we'd be living two hundred miles from the Arctic Circle the following year, in a trailer wedged in snow? It was as if I sensed that my experience of home would fly across the sky, drop with a thud to earth every so often, then lift up as if by a storm, as long as I lived with my parents.

4. Technicolor

A home requires a setting within and against which you define yourself; those regions you consider more "yours" than not. Yours not in ownership, necessarily, but in self-identification, the material world comprising some part of your own metaphorical body—the Freudian concept of *the extended self.*

How far can this self extend? Birds, animals, and insects make shelters out of an extraordinary range of materials from their habitats: the Tower of Babel–resembling anthills made of exquisitely chambered clay; beaver dams wrought of teeth-whittled wood, which account for the largest shelters made by nonhumans; birds' nests woven loosely with the twigs, foil, shredded paper, and string of an urban landscape. But only humans make a *variety* of housing, myriad architectures set in every possible environment, using materials that may be local or imported from very nearly anywhere. As a species, we've decided the world is our homeland, no exceptions: it's all ours.

Dorothy's farmhouse ripped out of its natural setting is no longer home to her. After all, she's within walking distance of her Kansas house the whole time she's in Oz, located there near the spiral starting point of the Yellow Brick Road. But her house does not function as her home if it's outside Kansas. Throughout her adventures in places far more alluring than a dusty gray plain, she repeats, "I have to get home to Kansas!"

I didn't have a root setting like this growing up. Most of my friends overseas had a home-back-home to yearn for. Instead, I set myself, had to, in Oz—a string of them. My family's mobile

homes may have all looked roughly the same, a déjà vu of
metal housing, but their doors opened onto three almost comically varied and dramatic environments, each possessing an
intensely singular climate and color scheme: white, gold, or
green.

5. Tundra

One trailer door opens to subarctic snowscape a hundred miles
north of Denali, where I walk to the yellow school bus with my
mother, who's bundled up in her green parka, my one-year-old
brother on her hip. White sheers around us—rivers, palaces,
frenzies of white, honed of frozen crystals. In the forest edging
our compound, I've seen a beaver dam domed high over rush-
ing waters that my dad said is an engineering marvel; I've seen
huskies with ice-blue eyes pull a man on a sled. My dad—all of
thirty-four, tall and slim, still in the handlebar mustache years—
left much earlier that morning for his job on the Trans-Alaska
Pipeline System's eight hundred miles of oil pipeline. I run
toward the bus, slip, fall into burning liquid: the whiteness has
cracked beneath my feet, and I'm submerged in a snow-buried
pond, my body—neck, scalp—clamped in ice water. Before I'm
pulled out, I thrash wildly, hear my own pulse like a fire alarm: a
base recognition of *heart*.

6. Desert

Another front door opens onto glass-bright heat, Arabian sunlight pouring across dunes, the sand silky as sugar, since this
desert has been at it a long time. My friend—a blue-eyed boy I
like—and I are riding our bikes on sand roads tire-marked by

backhoes, dump-trucks. In the distance toward the gulf, violet-blue flames flicker from the oil refinery towers shaped like taper candles, the industrial first stage of the petrochemical metropolis of Jubail—the largest engineering project in history, for which our fathers are employed. My friend and I drop our bikes, bound up the hump side of a dune, then roll down the smooth slip face—a heated, sifting, enveloping massage. Up close, the sand is a pointillism of seashell colors and now in our hair, ears, noses, mouths. The dunes move in fine patterned ripples and like massive buried animals. I'm fascinated by the desert's delicate yet sky-wide physics, this parallelism of *mind*.

7. Jungle

And the third trailer door opens in 1980 to damp glowing greenery deep in northeastern Colombia, a village with no power lines in the impoverished department of Córdoba. I'm ten and still a tomboy, busy building a fort with my friends, all girls, all wielding hammers and saws on leftover planks. We're shaded by heaving palms, a stretch of jungle we've learned from our schoolteacher is not rainforest, but what happens when a rainforest is felled for construction—mostly cattle ranches in Córdoba's case, over many centuries—its random surviving components shooting up like titanic weeds, and populated with bullfrogs larger than my head, cockroaches bigger than my hand, blue Morpho butterflies as electrically pigmented as airborne tropical fish. We've learned there are no gorillas here, just *guerrillas*—the FARC rebels just taking hold all around us. I've learned what cocaine is, what pot plants look like; that the best rum comes from Cuba, via Cartagena, a treacherous drive from our village. My dad's job involves a vast nickel strip-mine, and sometimes when he comes home, he passes out. Across the compound, in my family, I'm learning how illnesses and addictions sprout misshapen human forms: stagnant, overblown, out of whack. I learn what "too late" is, and what happens next; I learn—without meaning to—*courage*.

8. Tornado

When my son is ten, I realize he's never seen the movie version of *The Wizard of Oz*. I'd read him several Oz stories when he was about seven, and he'd proclaimed them his favorite books—a short-lived moment squelched by the oncoming narrative train of the Harry Potter series. Suspecting he may be too old to be truly dazzled, I make us popcorn and we sit down, my little family of three, for movie night.

The MGM lion roars, the opening credits flash across the stormy sky—and soon I'm surprised that the film's sepia-toned scenes draw me in so much more than Oz's jewel-box marvels. When I was a kid, I'd had the classic daydreamer's reaction: why hurry back to dreary old Kansas when you can live large over a glamorous, magical rainbow? More deeply, I'd never believed "there's no place like home," since my own idea of home was such a crazed moving target. But now I see it all differently: Professor Marvel's traveling fortune-teller's cart, the rounded Romani *vardo*, looks like a poignant ghost-ship of America's lost open roads. Aunt Em's reason and decency shine through, as does her wit—verbally smacking down evil Almira Gulch, but good. And then there's that famous final speech Dorothy gives to Glinda, words that will propel her—more than those ruby slippers—back to Kansas (and taken directly from L. Frank Baum's novel): "If I ever go looking for my heart's desire again, I won't look any further than my own backyard. Because if it isn't there, I never really lost it to begin with." I'd once loathed this speech as a false-ringing tribute to small-minded, small-town provincialism and checked out of the movie as soon as she made it. But now it strikes me as a gentle, life-saving prescription: *allow yourself*, you daydreaming Dorothys, to flourish in a place you name and consider your home.

Meanwhile, my son's movie review, in total: "It was pretty good! The Munchkins were cool." But what he loved, couldn't get over, asked questions about for days was the tornado. Are tornadoes ever that big? Can they just appear out of nowhere? Do they ever throw houses across the sky? Yes, I tell him, noticing how strange these facts actually are.

We talk about how every spring, hundreds of tornadoes hit Tornado Alley, a region winding from Minnesota down to Texas, where the world's highest percentage of tornadoes strike—and where mobile homes, usually only secured to the ground by concrete blocks and often the only residences affordable to lower-income people, are notoriously vulnerable to destruction.

He wants to see more tornadoes. So we watch a horrifying video of a supercell T5 tornado in Oklahoma tearing off a roof, lifting it as high as Dorothy's house seems to rise. We watch a news clip featuring the wreckage by another massive tornado, in which the top floor of a central Texas Holiday Inn was crushed by an upside-down double-wide trailer, stripped to its frame and chassis, its one last wheel poking into the sky.

9. Le Corbusier

Today you can buy a double-wide with ocean views in Malibu's Paradise Cove manufactured home park for $1.9 million; you can pick up a used mobile home for $20,000 on Craigslist, all utility lines intact; you can retire in comfort on a Florida golf course, in an age-restricted, upscale trailer resort. You could join the 20 million or so Americans who live in mobile homes.

What you can't do is find mobile homes listed in *6,000 Years of Housing*, the late architect Norbert Schoenauer's essential, beautiful, and world-spanning compendium of every form of housing imaginable, including all manner of mobile homes— tents, lean-tos, igloos, yurts. But there's no entry on mobile homes with chassis—that qualify, together, as the only home indigenous to the non-native United States in the architectural canon.

It's so quintessentially American, adding wheels and an engine's power to a primary residence—granting the conceptual freedoms of speed and exploration, to up and go wherever we like. But we may view this ability less charitably when it's enjoyed by *other* people. We can't just have everyone rolling around, parking and sleeping hither and yon: what would happen to neighborhoods, local governance, tax basis, social cohesion? Solid communities mean houses built on sturdy foundations. Or at least this has been our view of societal planning since our not-so-distant agrarian days, when being rooted to the land was no simile.

I'm still drawn to mobile homes, even the ones dismissed as "tin cans." I love the premise of a tighter, lighter footprint, the new versions powered by solar panels. But even the familiar, ready-made manufactured home—what we called a trailer— offers a simplicity that should get more respect. It's pared down, good for so many places and stages of life, like a pair of jeans.

Because to each of us, our home is always moving, whether now or in the past. This may not sound realistic, or practical, yet it is literal. Our experience of a place is always in flux,

because we live in it moving through time, trapped and enliv-
ened by its laws, our daydreams and memories breaking them
regularly.

So even when a person such as my partner, who grew up in
a normal number of childhood homes—three—looks back to
those places, they changed as he did, moved around him differently as he grew up.

When Le Corbusier said a home is "a machine for living in,"
I don't believe he's prescribing mechanization—that it should
be built of metal, say, its pieces winding around like a clock's—
but rather that he's speaking to this inherence of motion. The
machinery of life is aided not only by a working dishwasher but
by spaces for work, play, love, and rest. A home that doesn't
weigh or stifle but allows you to move through your life as you
desire, as you're capable of, is the only one worth living in.

10. Kansas

And so I've performed an experiment on my son. It involves his
entire life, has taken all of his ten years so far. Since I have one
child, he is my experiment's one shot.

My ground-shaking hypothesis: kids do better growing up
in one good, solid place than in many exciting, unpredictable,
strange, uncomfortable, sometimes wonderful, sometimes terrifying, one highly questionable, and nearly always confusing
ones.

To test my theory, we've lived in one house since my son was
an infant, a house that feels like some kind of tree. It doesn't
look like a tree—it's stucco, not wood-clad—but the rooted-
ness of the structure and our lives in it is completely novel to
me. I've never lived in one location for ten years. My longest
stint was five years in a West Village one-bedroom in my twen-

ties, one of three apartments during my decade in Manhattan. At 375 square feet, it functioned as a sprawling walk-in closet where I also happened to sleep and keep my coffeemaker. I considered my "home" to be New York, that pyrite-veined Emerald City, but never, until this house, did I consider an actual structure a home.

Guess what? It's working out. And I've noticed how our home contains myriad, ever-changing spaces for my son. In many ways, he's a designer, an engineer at heart, and he loves to rework his immediate world, building fort after fort all around the house for himself, his friends, his animals. Once, I found him building a fort *inside* his fort: the exterior for himself, and the interior for a cat, temporary homes that took shape like Russian nesting dolls.

My son's mobile homes move across the house and into the backyard. He builds them quickly out of blankets, chairs, pillows, cardboard boxes, bamboo poles, ballasts like a stack of books. Then he tears them down when they no longer serve their purpose: it's time to clean up his room, or his parents want to reclaim the living room couch. But he's already working out how to improve his design and is scouting the next location.

He builds his forts for an express purpose, and it's not to find a buyer or flip the forts for a profit. He builds them for the love and comfort of himself, his friends, his pets, and occasionally his mom, who bends herself small as she can to enter them. He offers a brief tour: entries and exits, places for sitting or lying down, where to watch my head. He hands me a flashlight and a book. Then he points to where the snacks are, a good host.

LIKELERS

1. Marin

I was fifteen and about to start junior year when my family
moved to Marin, county of scenic, moneyed bedroom communities across the Golden Gate Bridge from San Francisco.
It was 1985, and Marin was also still known for being—incom-
patibly, at first glance—a hippie countercultural capital, where
the Grateful Dead moved for good in 1970, inspiring many sta-
diums' worth of Deadheads to settle in the area. My family,
though, moved to one of Marin's least expensive or bohemian
parts: Terra Linda, an unincorporated enclave in the northern city of San Rafael. After many years living overseas or rent-
ing stateside, my forty-something parents were looking at the
starter house price range and could afford to buy there.

By any standard, Terra Linda is a nice place, though unlike
much of Marin, chichi or exclusive it is not. Yet its hilly sub-

urbs of tract housing developments possess two major architectural claims to fame. It features, for one, Frank Lloyd Wright's strangest, most surreal and otherworldly building, all qualities hidden in its workaday name: the Marin County Civic Center. It might look familiar to many of us today—even if we can't quite place it. More on this later.

Terra Linda is also home to nine hundred Eichlers—one of the largest collections of these prototypical midcentury houses, named for their creator, Joseph Eichler, a Manhattan-born builder and Frank Lloyd Wright devotee. Eichler revolutionized Californian architecture during the Cold War years by mass-producing modernist houses for middle-class homebuyers. Rare indeed among American developers, Eichler was driven by philosophy more than profit: he believed modernism's flexible, streamlined sensibility was inherently democratic and progressive and therefore should be accessible to all working people (literally so: he was among the first American builders who refused to "redline" tracts by race or ethnicity). By many accounts, Eichler believed his homes' uncluttered, open-plan designs could make people happier, that his communities would bring together like-minded groups.

And for a while they did. In the Bay Area of the 1950s and 1960s, Eichlers were where a well-educated populace of aerospace engineers, university professors, and other culturally elite but still middle-class Californians often wanted to live: 2,700 Eichlers were built in Palo Alto alone. But by the Summer of Love, Eichler's revolution of affordable, mildly futuristic design was over. Eichler Homes, his primary home-building company, filed for bankruptcy in 1967. And by the 1980s his namesake houses often had peeling paint and an abandoned air, considered hopelessly dated in that glitzy, wealth-flaunting decade.

So by the time my parents were looking to buy in Marin, Eichlers were near the lowest housing rung. But one was lower

still. Terra Linda also contains hundreds of fake Eichlers—
1960s-era knock-offs comically dubbed "Likelers." The gravel-
roofed house my parents bought was a Likeler—and my six-
teenth home.

During our house hunt, though, we toured a real Eichler for
sale in the Terra Linda flats. It was the first time I ever saw my
mother cry—or witnessed anyone brought to tears over a house.

2. Fixer

As my family drove up, all I could think was that the Eichler
looked like a big brown shoebox: flat-roofed and single story, its
plywood walls only windowed with opaque glass strips. So this
was "modernism," as my teenaged self was absorbing it: how
you might sketch a house in under, say, a strict seven-second
time limit.

We parked under the carport, and the realtor ushered us
inside with a mild warning: "Consider this a 'cosmetic fixer.'"
We stepped into a lava lamp in house form, a stage-set for acid
trips circa 1968. Walls gleaming kaleidoscopic patchwork
hues—purple, carnelian, fuchsia, banana yellow—were fes-
tooned with wiggly lined murals of towering magic mushrooms,
dragons and butterflies flying over rainbows and entwined
naked people, all in a goofy cartoon style I recognized from
Yellow Submarine. Turquoise shag carpeting curled up to our
ankles. The fug of cigarette and pot smoke—many, many years
of it—hung around us, as we stood there, staring.

"You can really smell the 'incense,'" murmured the realtor.
My dad chuckled. I smirked. My brother, age twelve, looked like
he'd rather be anywhere else on the planet.

"Wow," said my mom, in her crisp jeans and linen blouse, to
the stale air. "Ha ha!"

"The atrium has been cleared out," said the agent, pointing to the sliding glass door in the middle of the living room, where sunlight streamed into the courtyard beyond it. This feature is the highlight of the classic Eichler floor plan: the house, shaped like a rectangular donut, is centered around an open-air patio accessed through glass doors from all surrounding rooms. Eichler's signature and most beloved design element, these atriums popularized the concept of "bringing the outdoors in."

But we were all squinting hard at this atrium, its cracked cement patio smeared with sludgy water stains, so many rows of Dancing Bears stickers fused to the glass.

"It's a project, sure," said the realtor. "In the big picture, with refinished floors, some fresh paint, it's really not hard to . . ."

But my mother was running her hand across tinkly vines of colored beads where a door once hung and responded, "Ha ha!" She spotted the kitchen cabinetry painted a pop art flower scheme and repeated, "Ha ha!" Then her tight laughter swerved into tears, and she said, "I'm sorry, I don't think I can do this!" Her hands flew up to hide her face. My dad and the realtor startled, winced; then my dad put his arm around my mom and led her out the front door.

As my brother and I followed them to the car, I scrambled to understand what was happening. My parents had always been savvy people, as parents went—down to earth, open-minded, unruffled by much. So the house was a "project," sure, but how was it worth tears? My family drove away in silence—and we immediately pretended the crying never happened.

We later joked, though, about that "psychedelic Eichler." Thanks to my parents' fond if satirical explanations of Marin County, I knew the decor embodied an aging stereotype of hippie fantasia, a time capsule of the "peacock feathers and hot tubbing" Marin before all the really rich people moved there, and the yuppies. But that tuned-in, turned-on, dropped-out old Marin was a place my parents had no interest in inhabiting, never mind cleaning up. Did my mother cry from the disappointment that *this*—this whacked-out possible home—was what her life had come to, like a silly and annoying penance for her and my dad's own alternative choices? After all, as globe-trotting expats, they'd been in no hurry to settle down in the suburbs.

But that "psychedelic Eichler" amazed me: It was a place where people had literally lived out their dream lives, had re-created a dreamworld in reality. So it was a crazy dream, to my eye—but aren't most dreams, if they're worth remembering? The LSD-styled decor struck me as hilarious, brave, and entirely stupid looking. But it wasn't any stupider looking than the beige walls everyone else in the 1980s seemed to dream of, the shiny brass fixtures of the era, the ubiquitous puffy faux leather recliners, the spider plants hanging in the kitchen. Beige walls and spider plants: what kind of dream did that speak of? The dream where nothing happens, small repetitive irritating dreams, so inconsequential and dull we rarely mention them. The best thing we could say of such dreams: at least they aren't nightmares.

Being fifteen and in many ways fortunate, I thought you could always wake up from a nightmare.

But even then, I saw how two conflicting American dreams slammed together in that house: Eichler's one-size-fits-all modernism, built for an idealized calm and enlightened middle-class, for Californian men like my dad with nice mechanical pencils in their front pockets and gainful office jobs. The interior was hijacked by full-bore hippies circa late 1960s and 1970s Marin, heyday and headquarters of unbridled self-expression—as long as your self loved large quantities of drugs and Day-Glo colors. In the coming years, my dad will meet many survivors of this scene in his Marin County AA meetings, a Who's Who of talented and well-known local musicians, artists, and writers, all working the program so that they, like my dad, could stay alive.

But this being 1985, both those dreams were over. The eighties were in full glaring swing, its mainstream bits epitomized by trickle-down Reaganomics and Madonna's all-too-obvious "Material Girl," by the "value" that living well was the best revenge. But what, other than having lots of money, did living well mean? My family didn't have lots of money; could we live well in Marin? I wasn't sure where we had landed, how to understand this place. What good had survived from the past in my new hometown, and what dreams mattered now—to us?

3. Democracy

On one side of Highway 101 stands a timeworn A&W and a gas station. On the other, a pyramidal gold spire twists upward, narrowing into a sixteen-story-tall needle. Brilliant sky-blue domes and coved rooflines float around it like inverted pools and lagoons in a green forest. These stretches of cerulean, etched like sea shells, top terra cotta buildings carved with hundreds of round windows and arches that run the length of several stories. Futuristic and Moorish, alien and Californian, the complex resembles a ravishing science fiction cityscape.

This is Frank Lloyd Wright's Marin County Civic Center—his last building and his only federal government project. Wright never saw it: ground broke in 1960, the year after he died at age ninety-one. But he considered it a breakthrough in his "architecture of democracy," one representing a society's best possible future and arising from its natural setting. In Wright's aesthetic, gone are classical Western tropes of Greek columns and Italian Renaissance domes; the new buildings of

American governance would provide a view facing forward in time, from inspirations wrought only of their localities.

So amid subdivisions and freeway, Wright's notion of local democracy is embodied as a fantastical oasis.

When my family moved to Terra Linda, we toured the busy Civic Center on a rainy day. As harried-looking people made their way to the Public Works Department or the Hall of Justice, water rivulets streaked the damp atriums, collecting in mossy pools. My dad explained that Wright's architecture sometimes worked like this: so striking from a distance, it could appear uneven up close, dank or fractured with cracks, thanks to the classic design problem of valuing form over function. Rainwater leaks had long plagued the interior rooms. We wandered down the long, beautiful, damp balconies scalloped with open-air archways, corridors perhaps too exposed to the elements to be practical.

But so what? This is American democracy as built landscape. Upkeep is ongoing; renovations will be required. The structure is so brilliant, it is worth any nitty-gritty work, the larger vigilance. Wright's revelatory visualization of government architecture—so unlike anything in D.C. or Philadelphia or any State Capital, USA—is a sight, a place, more of us should experience. It's freeing. It invites confidence and creativity.

And in fact, we can all glimpse a plumped and softened version of Wright's masterpiece in *Star Wars: Episode 1, The Phantom Menace*, the 1999 movie Generation Xers like me seem to universally despair of, after adoring the brazenly thrilling 1970s Star Wars movies as kids. George Lucas, a longtime nearby resident, reimagined Wright's Marin County Civic Center as Padmé Amidala's palace on Naboo, an airbrushed utopia of reason, politesse, and democratic process: the complex of sky-blue domes and terra cotta archways where Natalie Portman strolls, pondering Very Important Senate Rules.

For all its cool splendor, the Marin County Civic Center hosts the most workaday goings-on of local government and bureaucracy, the chores for which we citizens grit our teeth. As a teenager, I liked to think it was Wright's little joke to make going to the post office or clearing up an unpaid parking ticket like visiting an outer-space cathedral on acid.

But now, in 2018, I see—very literally—what Wright was doing: designing a vision of democracy's future for which we will never stop having use. Such place-specific, adventurous building should be commonplace in America, and his example has never looked more relevant or ingenious. It's a better world set right here, even in the suburbs, in our own back yards.

4. Terra Linda

My family's Likeler stood on high on a hill north of the civic center, along a road dead-ending at preserved lands. Another shoe box–shaped house, it featured a gravel roof and dark interior circa 1961, the year it was built. My parents' plan was to renovate and resell it—"flipping" was not yet a term—so they could use the profit to buy a house we could afford to own permanently. So when we moved in, I knew we'd be leaving soon. I knew not to get attached to this place. And this place, the setting itself, was among the most stunning I'd seen. I was not alone in this: Wright called these hillsides "one of the most beautiful landscapes."

"Terra Linda" sounds like it dates to California's deep Mexican past, translating from Spanish to "beautiful land"—which does sum it up: long grassy hills and valleys, studded with live oaks and pewter serpentine outcroppings, shimmer green or gold in the two-toned, wet or dry seasons. To the southwest rise expansive views of Marin's mesmerizing highest peak, Mount

Tamalpais, which provides an uncanny object of meditative stillness, tipped and flowing toward the Pacific Ocean a few miles west like a high-cresting wave in a Japanese painting.

Yet "Terra Linda" has shallow and Portuguese roots. The name was dreamed up in the 1950s by the daughter of the land's Azores-born owner, the wildly successful entrepreneur Manuel T. Freitas, a dishwasher-turned-banker who founded a financial institution that later would be absorbed into the Bank of America. Freitas wanted to sell off his dairy farmland, and with the help of daughter Rose, Terra Linda was born and bought up by housing developers—including Joseph Eichler. Another builder, Patrick Tennant, purchased a tract to construct thirty-one houses in 1959. His native County Kerry village would inspire the perplexing name of our otherwise nondescript street.

Knocknaboul is an Irish moniker that I now know translates to "hilltop and field," but in 1985, we had no idea what it meant. My dad joked it was Gaelic for "tract house." In local newspaper articles from 1961, Tennant explained that Terra Linda recalled his native western Ireland's lush, rock-strewn landscape. Nevertheless, a disgruntled original resident asked the county to change "Knocknaboul Way" to the bland but pronounceable "Sandalwood Drive." But Tennant petitioned most of the tract's homeowners to defend the ethnic flare. "Those Irish stick together," sighed a county supervisor when the name was kept.

Tennant was only the latest Irishman to leave his mark. Back in 1898, Manuel Freitas had bought his tract from Irish rancher John Lucas, for whom the neighboring San Rafael area of Lucas Valley is named. This has led to widespread confusion for Marinites, since Lucas Valley is where George Lucas has long lived and for decades ran his filmmaking empire. In 1978 he began buying up the redwood-threaded valley to build Skywalker Ranch and the campus for Industrial Light and Magic. By the eighties, many assumed that Lucas Valley was named after George Lucas. I believed it. Why not?

And anyway, John Lucas had merely been sole heir to a rich uncle: the legendary Irish Mexican settler Don Timoteo Murphy. In 1844 the Mexican governor granted Murphy twenty-two thousand acres—including today's Terra Linda and adjacent Lucas Valley—for raising Spanish steer. Massive in stature at six feet, two inches, and three hundred pounds, noted to be "more king than don," Murphy was famous for his huge parties where he would serve bear he himself had killed. He was known for being "fair" to the native people, at least according to other Mexican settlers.

These indigenous inhabitants would have been Miwok people, whose coast tribe had lived in the area for thousands of years. Their language gives us both "Marin" and "Tamalpais." Few place-names so perfectly elide sound with subject.

So notions and memories, transparencies and visions of Mexico, Spain, Ireland, Portugal, and Miwok culture all jostle in the atmosphere and Creole of the hills.

And so much of any place—America, California, Marin County, anywhere—contains similar collective overlays, meanings made up, mistranslated, riffed and repainted by imagination and will. So much of *place* is experienced as resemblances, resonances with our personal elsewheres, alongside those of everyone around us, as they fit into the larger landscape, its favorite-told histories. We build our lives right on top of them.

5. Jerry's Daughter

I was always leaving our Terra Linda house, the Likeler my mom did not like. Her complaints weren't unfounded. Our house possessed no character, sure; it had weirdly small windows and low ceilings, true. But what did any of that matter to me? I'd started at a new high school—another Catholic one—as an incoming junior and was relieved about one thing: my chance to renovate myself.

At my previous school, I'd been a cheerleader, class president, and homecoming princess: your basic nightmare. I'd worked hard to be popular, but with success, I then felt fake. I didn't have the perspective to know that fifteen-year-olds generally feel like this and that human beings often do, no matter how old they get. When my family moved to Marin, I vowed I'd stop with the status-chasing and people-pleasing and figure out what I loved and who I actually was. But for the first months at Marin Catholic, I was merely the new girl navigating strangers' social groups, trying to figure out where I belonged. Not with the football crowd or its cheerleaders—no more pom-poms for me—but otherwise, I was open to all of it.

And by the time I got home from school, whether exhausted or exhilarated by the day, all I wanted was to escape my new house with its too-small windows and too-low ceilings, my mother's endless projects to improve it. I'd put on my Walkman and walk to the end of Knocknaboul Way, where protected open hillsides began. I'd hike the deer paths, listening to tapes of Kate Bush or New Order or the Smiths, Talking Heads or the English Beat or Style Council, carried along by the music. I loved how the place was a dead ringer for Ireland, where I'd visited as a kid and had gleaned was a world headquarters for wordsmiths and music lovers. But Terra Linda's sharp-carved hills and circus tent–sized oak trees and rock formations shimmered under balmy skies, casting fine-spun warmth across the skin—as if a perfect Mediterranean climate had wandered over to Galway.

In the coming months, those walks reshaped something

deep in me: anytime I felt lost or bored or wanted more, new ideas about writing and music kept rising to meet me. The landscape reminded me of what could make people happy, even if only by association, my own projections of "Ireland" and its arts, handily reincarnated as topography at the end of my street.

And in Marin music grew everywhere and in every form, like a botanical garden of performers. I knew the Grateful Dead had cleared the way, that Jerry Garcia himself lived in San Rafael. Adolescently proud of my post-punk tastes, I was no Deadhead. But in truth I'd listen to almost anything because music itself proved magical, reshaping any place, any moment with invisible emotional architectures. And anyway, moving to Marin in the eighties and tuning out the Grateful Dead would be like moving to Rome and ignoring Catholicism.

So I was excited to see Bobby Weir—well, he *looked* like Bobby Weir—coming out of the 7-Eleven in Fairfax. And also Huey Lewis in his Mercedes stopped at a red light, waving as my friends and I ogled him from the next car. And Grace Slick looking like a French actress in a Mill Valley cafe. And Journey's Steve Perry ducking into the back of a car in downtown San Rafael, outside the club he owned.

One day for lunch, my friend and I were eating in her car outside Togo's, and she said, "Look, there's Jerry's Daughter!" A teenage girl our age walked by. My friend explained that she went to San Rafael High, which I knew was where 420 had started: code for getting stoned, as the burnouts did there every afternoon at 4:20. But Jerry's Daughter didn't look like a burnout, just a regular, non-stoner teenager. Just like us. It was thrilling, this musical royalty, this normalcy.

The following year, Camper Van Beethoven released "We Saw Jerry's Daughter" because of course the experience deserved its own song. By that point I was spending all my part-time job money on thrift store clothes—velvet jackets, leather skirts, stompy boots—and concert tickets. I was close enough to "the City"—what San Francisco so cleverly got itself to be called by its suburbs—to go to shows, in all the clubs and concert halls I loved, with my tribe of Golden Gate Bridge–driving teenagers.

The city/suburb cultural split did Terra Linda no favors in my mind. I now predictably saw suburbs as pretend places, make-believe kid-centric toy towns, which you must leave to find someplace "real." And this was embodied in my own dull, comfortable house, which I'd come to view as a trap for my family, where none of us felt at home.

6. Eichlers

Before he became a homebuilder, Joseph Eichler rented the Bazett House, one of Frank Lloyd Wright's Usonian-style homes in Hillsborough, California, for several years during World War II. Usonians were the rare smaller homes Wright designed for middle-class budgets. Eichler was forty-eight years old, unemployed after decades as a produce salesman, and wondering what career to take on next.

The Usonian demonstrated for Eichler the emotional, psychological, and transformative power of architecture, and in doing so changed his life. The sleek, open design aesthetic—flat roof, clerestory windows, myriad skylights and glass walls—made Eichler and his wife feel content, peaceful, yet energized. How could architecture do this? To Eichler the house showcased and magnified three visceral pleasures of retreat: light and nature and privacy. As the years passed, he grew inspired to *democratize* Wright's bespoke, custom-built, and in practice very pricey Usonians. He would make Wright's "middle-class" modernist-style houses actually affordable to the middle class.

How to keep costs down? Eichler and his architects would base their designs on post-and-beam construction, where all structural weight is born by these skeletal frames—freeing the walls to be built of light, inexpensive materials. So if an Eichler's front exterior looks constructed of little more than plywood, that's because it's constructed of little more than plywood.

When I revisited Terra Linda this year, the street of Eichlers I wandered down felt eerily abandoned, even for the suburbs. The nearly windowless front expanses give the houses a collectively gloomy air, like they've been walled in or shuttered up. Eichler design represents the suburban ethos made extreme, visually literal: a turning away from the city and its rigamarole, from people and their gazes, a going inward into privacy, that walled garden. It's extreme introversion as architecture.

Step inside a classic Eichler to understand its appeal. At its best, the interior resembles a stark jewel-box of natural light. Glass walls open onto landscaped, high-fenced backyards, or around a family room–sized central atrium. Eichlers reincarnate an ancient ideal of domestic architecture, refreshingly un-American, one recalling Moorish and Spanish Mexican housing: The exterior is intentionally plain; the beauty, charm, and finishes are saved for the interior. And indoors contains the outdoors: views and patios graced with the plants and atmospheres of California's temperate climate.

Like all modernist architecture, Eichlers look best nearly empty. Psychedelic hippie decor, the usual family tchotchkes, or really any sign of personality other than ascetic or midcentury modern may not work. The Eichler *embodies* an ethos of spare, chic modesty. Eichler himself understood that this style hid the homeowners from view as much as it represented them, appealing to his original customer base of bright, offbeat people unmoved by the conspicuous consumptions of mainstream American culture.

Above all, Eichler believed his homes' multifunctional, naturally luminous design could make people happy. This is, really, an extraordinary assertion. Does architecture, even in a form as personal as a home, have the power to make people happy? How much of life depends on the stage on which it happens?

What I learned from our Likeler was that houses could make people unhappy. And by "people," I mean my mother. The house became a barometer of both my parents' discontent with their finances, their place in the world, but it was my mother's complaints I heard. Happiness seemed an unrelated matter. It was the degree of unhappiness about our status that the house seemed to measure.

On the weekends, my dad refinished the hardwood floors, updated lighting fixtures, enlarged windows. My mother planned everything, painted the walls a creamy white, hung spider plants in the kitchen. They readied the Likeler for its future open house. Until that day, it represented for them a giant to-do list of improvements.

The only dream my parents had for our Likeler was to make money from it. It looked like a home, but it was something else, a generator of monetary wealth, and as such, we would have been fools to imbue it with deeper personal meaning. It was an object.

So my parents commodified the very sanctuary home represents—in the long, common, and incessant tradition of American strivers. It's everyday practice now, but it's always been fueled by anxieties surrounding class. According to my mom, the "middle class" encompassed adults with high school degrees and good jobs. "Upper middle class" was our supposed echelon, designated by my parents' higher education and white-collar career income. My mother seemed to think Terra Linda was too regular middle class, and one source of her discontent was that we still couldn't afford it.

When I ask my mom about the Likeler today, to my surprise she says quietly, "I wish we could have stayed there."

We all have our snobberies. And if we are not rich or striving to be—or want to be seen as such—many of them work in reverse.

7. Gardens

Steve Jobs used to tell reporters that he'd grown up in an Eichler in Palo Alto. He said the house inspired his ideas about the interactive beauty of clean, lucid minimalism—ideas that would fundamentally shape his Apple product design aesthetic, epitomized in the sleek, intuitive, beautifully lit iPhone. But then a reporter dug up the history of Jobs's former house and revealed that Jobs was mistaken. It was no Eichler but was, instead, a Likeler.

Nevertheless, the "Steve Jobs grew up in an Eichler" legend lives on and is one small reason Eichlers in Palo Alto are no longer affordable to the middle class. The larger reason is the local decimation of the middle class itself. My family had lived in Silicon Valley just before moving to Marin, and in the 1980s middle-class people regularly worked as computer programmers for tech firms like IBM. The era of widespread employee stock option deals bequeathing spiky riches was yet to come.

Today, Eichlers fetch millions in the Palo Alto market, thanks to the nearby Facebook, Google, and Apple corporate campus trifecta, which walls in the super-wealthy socioeconomic city-state of today's Silicon Valley. Eichlers are the rare older homes that may not be torn down for new mansions but are instead painstakingly renovated. These houses represent one ethos of the Bay Area's new rich, reflecting their extreme affluence, yes, but also their restrained tastefulness and relative enlightenment. For these tech millionaires, Eichlers embody Silicon Valley's futurism-loving "history," and so are the perfect, Steve Jobs–sanctioned, upper-class status symbols. This represents a complete misunderstanding or overlooking of Eichler's mandate to make modernist architecture accessible to middle-class Americans.

But in California, in this country, we're not sure who or where the middle class is anymore. Tech workers and their satellite professions have drifted upward in economic status, at sudden, unprecedented multiples of income. But this wealth-heavy elite means that so many more people, in direct competition for the same housing and services, are being pushed downward.

My dream of California remains rooted in the cultures of Mexico and the Mediterranean, with peoples who value the life of the senses: the arts and crafts they inspire, the changeable colors and textures of outdoor living. California for me is a dream of the sensual, of experimentation, of sex appeal, however quirky, and therefore not to be obsessively quantified, cold-splashed awake by the mining and crunching and monetizing of endless data. But my dream is of a place vanishing before my eyes. This California loses more every minute to the digital mainstream, its grindingly massive wealth, the skewed values of virtual realities. California is famous for its booms and busts, true, but this boom really seems different. It doesn't involve gold or silver enriching local coffers; its Silicon has already changed the world.

I revisited my family's old Likeler this year. After I drove over from my home in dense, quasi-urban Berkeley, I was struck by the beauty and tranquility of Terra Linda's valleys. The house looked eerily the same, as if I'd time-traveled to the day my parents sold it, their eyes now on the next flip. They would never settle anywhere. The Likeler seemed to fade from my view: the apotheosis of forgettable, generic tract housing. As always, I left it fast. I walked to the end of the road, chose Kate Bush from my iPhone, and headed back into the protected public lands, the dream of those hills. It's still a garden anyone can cultivate.

DADAHOLIC

> The cloud clears as you enter it.
>
> —BERYL MARKHAM,
> *West with the Night*

1. Insatiable

I think a lot about how I'm going to tell my son, now eleven, how my dad died. I've laid some groundwork. I introduced the word *alcoholic* a couple of years ago: special people, alcoholics, very special! These special alcoholic people can't, because of their genetics, their DNA (my son was looking at me now, since DNA models fascinate him), they can't handle drinking alcohol in a moderate way.

"What's alcohol?" he'd asked. *Oh, right*, I thought.

Alcohol, I told him, is a powerful type of drink because it makes people *feel* so different: sometimes calmer, or sillier, or happier, or sadder, or crazier, depending on the person and how much they have. Wine is one type of alcohol, beer is another. (He shrugged as if to say, "So alcohol is just wine.") It's a drink, but it's also a *drug*, and that's what makes it powerful. Drinking a small amount—like your dad and I do, and only because we're adults!—is okay for a lot of people.

But alcoholics, I told him, have a kind of allergy to alcohol, like your friends with the really bad nut allergies. At this his eyes widened; nut allergies are serious, even deadly. I went on: Only when the alcoholic starts drinking alcohol, they can't stop, so it's like an allergy in reverse. *All they want* is alcohol. And if anyone drinks too much alcohol—whether over time, or all at once—that person will die.

He nodded. I could tell it made sense to him. It made sense to me at that moment.

But really it made no sense at all.

What part of the genome is this, exactly, that trips off the inability to not get plastered? How does one drink lead someone immediately to ten, according to genes? Where even the scent of alcohol can create an insatiable desire to consume it? Because that's what my dad used to say was true of him.

As a child in the 1970s and 1980s, I was raised to understand alcoholism as a disease, an illness as congenital and genetically determined as, say, type 1 diabetes. And like diabetes, alcoholism required careful dietary management. In short: No alcohol allowed. None. After my dad stopped drinking when I was around my son's age, we were a completely dry house.

Yet I now realized, after my wobbly, semi-sensical explanation, that I had no idea if this was how alcoholism was defined anymore. I'd long ago lost the thread on alcoholism as a breaking science news story. What's the latest? What treatment philosophy is all the rage? Are there drugs to help? Of course there must be drugs to help, no doubt a whole lucrative alcoholism-treating drug industry.

None of that touched me now. I lost my father to his alcoholism in 1997, and his death had carved out an emptied, time-stopped place inside me, a place familiar to anyone who has

loved someone who died by suicide. This inward state of noth-
ingness, this core-burrowed hole, is sometimes called *devasta-
tion*. It's a pretty useful word, as pain words go, for describing
the sheer complete utter gutting cureless sense of loss. And it's
pain you learn to live with, fallow ground you bury in your life,
hopefully tending new regions madly around it. What could
have grown there? Who knows.

But somehow, at some point, I will have to explain my
father's death to my son. And there's so much to get wrong
here: about drinking, about alcoholism, about our family, and
most of all about my dad.

Because here's the really tricky part, the twist that alcoholic
dad stories often do not have: I liked my dad, and was under the
distinct impression he liked me. During all the years he was
sober, we'd hang out, my dad and me. We'd listen to music.
We took drives, just to look at a view and grab some lunch.
He gave me good, thoughtful advice during all his sober years.
As father-daughter relationships go, I knew I'd had a great one
with him: respectful and fond, helpful and fun.

Then he began drinking again and didn't stop.

2. Meetings

It was in Alakids in the 1980s that I'd realized how unusual my
family seemed, even set within the highly secretive, variously
dysfunctional universe of alcoholic families.

My dad had just gotten out of a six-week session in an alcoholism treatment center in Redwood City, California. This
capped off what had been my family's craziest year, my sixth
grade: we'd been living in a Colombian jungle on a massive
engineering project when my dad's secret alcohol addiction
began affecting his job performance for the first time in his

career. My brother and I, growing up, never saw our dad drinking or drunk in a way we would recognize; in Colombia I only noticed him sleeping more. Finally, my mom announced that my dad had contracted malaria, a disease so scary and famous it allowed us to move to California for medical care. But this "malaria" turned out to be a lie concocted by kind, select coworkers to give my dad a chance to sober up privately. And so, once we arrived in the Bay Area, my dad entered the treatment center, while my mom, my brother, and I lived with my grandparents in their Silicon Valley home.

After those six weeks of facing his addiction, my dad moved back in with us. He sat my brother and me down, explained what an alcoholic was, that he was one, and that he would control his desire to drink by talking to other alcoholics a few times a week in something called "meetings"—made all the more powerful by their magical vagueness.

Then we got a taste of those meetings. They were held at night at a Catholic school not far from the Catholic school I'd just started at as a seventh grader. While my parents split off to the AA and Alanon rooms, my brother and I were sent to Alakids meetings. My mom voiced her doubts about this—who knew what tales of abuse we'd be exposed to?—but she had to go sit in the Alanon room, so maybe it was only fair. Hers was clearly the worst room, hosting the most visibly depressed, teary, and furious.

And no wonder: Alanon people, the partners, the parents, the best friends of alcoholics, had no control over their loved-one's drinking, but—worse!—they had to *admit* they had no control. No more cover-ups, denial, excuses, or savior complexes; instead, they had to face up to a cold, stupid, actually happening reality they could not influence. As all humans know, this is the very least fun thing to do: Much better to keep plowing ahead using all our old tricks! Meanwhile, my dad, the star of the night, strode to the main tent, the AA room, which involved regular comedy routines, if the shouts of laughter emanating from it were any indicator. He always seemed buoyant afterward, and so relieved.

The Alakid room was run by a young adult guy I loathed instantly and for ungracious reasons, for his long stringy hair, super-eager smile, and ceaseless probing questions. He wanted us to "go around the circle" (ugh!) and talk about how we felt about the drinking in our families. Why did I have to tell these strangers anything about my family or my feelings? It struck me as lunacy to even want to. And what would I say? My dad used to drink secretly, but we, his family, only just found out about that. Now he was sober and liked AA. Problem solved! It did not make for compelling storytelling.

By contrast, the first-to-talk volunteers were two sisters who lived with their monstrous alcoholic father. He was unemployed, they said, and sat around drinking and watching TV all day. He occasionally flew into violent rages, smashing his fists into them or their mother. And they didn't have enough money for new shoes. While the moderator acted like he'd heard this story before (Classic Alcoholic Dad Saga Number 1?), I stared at their flip-flops, wondering with horror, *Shouldn't we call the police and get these girls out of there? Abuse is illegal, right?* By contrast, my dad was nicely employed; nobody in my family got hit, under any circumstances; I had plenty of shoes. Compared to these girls, I had not a thing to complain about.

I looked up at the classroom walls where the students' names were listed: Theresa, Patrick, Steve, Lisa. There were Theresas and Patricks and Steves and Lisas at my new school. Panic arose as I realized that I had entered a parallel universe of Catholic schools: by night in one, I was expected to discuss murky, embarrassing family secrets; by day in another, all I wanted was to fit in as a normal kid.

MOBILE HOME

I resolved, right then, to never talk about alcoholism anywhere. After all, they couldn't actually *make* me. While we may be an "alcoholic family," we were not the traumatic, abusive, apparently textbook kind. And my dad, I reasoned, already had his drinking under control.

When it came my turn in the go-around-the-circle of hell, I mumbled something about Colombia, and everyone looked confused ("You were living in a *jungle*?"). Then I said, because I believed it: "There's not much to talk about." The moderator pressed for details, but I shook my head. My little brother looked bright-eyed with relief and, next up, skipped his turn.

A few weeks later, my mother had had enough of the Ala-non room. From then on, my dad was the only one who went to meetings. And he did, several times a week. For the next thirteen years, Alcoholics Anonymous meetings helped my father stay sober.

3. Adult Children

If you're an adult child of an alcoholic, you may find yourself picking up *Children of Alcoholism: A Survivor's Manual*. It's the classic on the subject, written by Judith S. Seixas and Geraldine Youcha, who together coined the phrase "Adult Children of Alcoholics"—which, while not a term that pushes the bounds of creativity, is useful nonetheless.

After thirteen years of sobriety, my dad started drinking again sometime after moving to Algeria. (Yes, he was living in Algeria.) This was 1995, when he was employed on a challenging, isolated engineering project there, while my mother stayed in the States. He fell ill with a virulent ear infection that rendered him deaf and with severe tinnitus in one ear and hearing impaired in the other. His company flew him to London, but treatment didn't work. He was released from the hospital, labeled "physically disabled"—mostly because of the severity of the tinnitus, a constant loud ringing in the ear—and placed on disability. At this point, fearing the loss of his successful career, my dad began drinking.

I was living in Manhattan as a freelance writer, getting panicked phone calls from my mom saying she couldn't reach my dad. Then an old family friend in London visited my dad in his hotel and reported to my mom that my dad was drinking, heavily. That's why he wasn't answering her calls, though he'd be flying home in a couple of days. I couldn't believe this was happening, even as a sinking fear took hold. I wondered when I would sleep again.

As an Adult Child of an Alcoholic, I needed some help. I bought the "survivor's manual" and opened, naturally, to the first chapter—which offers a section called "Incest." Holy hell, I thought, what's this? Seixas and Youcha recount a painful, terrifying story of a woman who'd been repeatedly raped as a girl by her monstrous alcoholic father. I felt a piercing if helpless compassion and understood, intellectually, that the book addressed many types of alcoholic parents. But my particular father never molested me or anyone else. Sure, he drank, but he wasn't a sexual predator or a psychopath. I felt, in that raw moment of my own, like the kitchen sink had been thrown at me. I closed the book.

My dad's abuse was never directed at us, his family. My dad's abuse was directed only at himself.

What I'd needed help with was the unfolding self-destruction of someone I loved. And I needed it for the next two years, as my dad, back in the States, checked himself into five different alcohol treatment centers, then continued drinking after each and every one.

4. Father Figure

A woman who was close to her father often gets dubbed a Daddy's Girl. Over the years, I've heard many women call themselves this, in proof of how loved they were by their fathers.

I was close to my father. But I was not a Daddy's Girl.

And I find the whole concept a little creepy.

To be fair, we don't have many models to choose from on the subject of fathers and daughters, other healthier frameworks or dynamics. And maybe it's an unanswered question at this point: what does a father mean to his daughter in the modern developed world, outside the stereotypical rules of traditional patriarchy? Countless novels, children's books, and Hollywood movies still depict the daughter as a princess, needing to get Daddy's approval to either marry the man she loves or to convince him not to marry her off to the wrong guy. As far as conservatively Christian cultures go, anyone who reads the New Testament will see that not much can budge there. Paul's letters to the Ephesians, written as they were in the Iron Age, make very clear that the father is the head of the family, the godhead on earth, and must be obeyed by his wife and kids.

I come from a family of thoughtful non-deists and common-sense egalitarians. There was no talk of "godheads" or the submission of women to their fathers or husbands or anyone else. So if we subtract out this religious framework—the one that gets us everything from your run-of-the-mill women-can't-be-leaders sexism to the watered-down bumbling-dad Americanized patriarchy typified in movies like *Father of the Bride*—what positive role does a father play in his daughter's life? Other than being the older guy who grumbles about writing big checks for her fancy wedding? As she, always depicted as a blandly pretty cipher, giggles, "Oh Daddy," before flouncing off to discuss the flower order with the wedding consultant. She is princess to his king, forever his little girl.

Consider, in the realm of fathers raising daughters, a different model.

Ally. Strategist. Ally and strategist in a world that wants her to submit to things that are not good for her, for any human being with intelligence, ambition, and self-respect. This is the support she can use: battle tactics. How to develop a strong offense, a clever defense, in a series of battles too often stacked against her. A teacher in maneuvers for the long game.

Meg, don't be afraid to stand up for yourself.
Stay focused, and you can write your own ticket.
You can do anything you set your mind to.

5. Model

Not long after my dad stopped drinking in California, I vaulted through puberty and emerged, through no effort of my own, with body measurements *Seventeen* magazine said were ideal for bikini wear. Meanwhile, my face realigned so that my features evened out, my cheekbones suddenly jutting photogenically. By the time I was fourteen, nearly everywhere I went, strangers said, "You should model!" Or, to my parents, "She should model!"

I knew this was nonsense. But I was startled, even stunned by my body's seismic shift into sex object. I'd been a math-loving bookworm kid, adept at standardized tests, and my dad counseled me to become an engineer when I grew up: *Get a degree in engineering, then an MBA, and you can write your own ticket.* But now I felt like I'd won the world's most indistinct, antifeminist lottery. I had no idea what any of it meant on a practical level—other than getting more attention? but almost always the

dumbest, cheapest kind?—or why I had to carry my winnings
around with me, like just standing there Being Very Pretty
was equivalent to flipping through stacks of hundreds in people's faces. It was gauche. It was garish. Yet everyone seemed to
admire it, even as some seemed to hate me on sight for it.

My mother, a Beautiful Woman in the Elizabeth Taylor
mold, worried me by how often I now caught her staring at me.

But my dad saw my discomfort, annoyance, and occasional
shame over all the stares. He was matter-of-fact about the whole
thing.

"People are going to look at you, Meg. Not much you can do
about it," he'd say. "Just remember your best feature," finger
tap to the temple, "is up here."

6. Bands and Films

When I was in seventh grade, my parents gave me a little boom-
box and my dad made me a tape. He recorded a copy of *The
Beatles, 1967–1970* from his original cassette. He wrote out the
songs on the plastic box cover sheet in his cool, lovely, sharp
yet swirly script. It's a rare piece of his wonderful handwrit-
ing I still have. Nostalgia for record albums is rampant now, but
here's a less-mentioned nostalgia: the handwritten song titles
on a cassette tape someone made for you.

So the Beatles songs came at me as a compilation, no albums
to make sense of the interior narratives or chronology. Now I
understand that *Abbey Road* is the greatest Beatles album, that
Sergeant Pepper's Lonely Hearts Club Band broke a novel and
a symphony into rock and roll, but back then I loved having the
songs in one place. I listened to that tape—I'm guessing—hundreds of times. If there was a spiritual tradition for my father,
some kind of higher meaning we could talk about openly, it

seemed to involve the Beatles: the wit, the inviting innovation, the sheer geometric beauty of those songs.

He preached and I testified that "Hey Jude" was the best Beatles song, among a dozen genius contenders, because it broke the rules the others perfected. It alone could make me tear up, even though I didn't really understand why. My dad talked about the repetition, the circling back of the lyrics and melody, the building to the crescendo, and then the wild sprawling hypnotic raucous spell of that finale. He was talking about a song; he was talking about the mechanics of joy in this world.

MTV appeared that same year, 1982, and I, at age twelve, was instantly riveted by music videos. Some of MTV's original featured songs were clearly terrible, but I didn't care: I would stare, dazzled, until someone made me stop. A couple of years later, my dad and I began watching a local alternative music video show. It featured bands from my beloved college radio stations, and yes, I watched it with my dad. We had our favorites: "Why?" by Bronski Beat, "Save It for Later" by the English Beat, "Blue Monday" by New Order, many other songs by British post-punk bands that defined one bright strand of the decade's music.

And soundtracks packed with "New Wave" were the primary reason I adored John Hughes movies. How did Hughes, a dreaded Baby Boomer, get the music of young suburban Gen Xers exactly right?

Teenage movies from the 1980s have been reassessed of late for a variety of sins, and rightfully so. But I noticed, even back then, how the fathers in those films were often so supportive of their daughters: That final scene in *Sixteen Candles* when Molly Ringwald's muddled, overlooked dad suddenly signals for her to stop being so "helpful"—and instead go for what she wants (a cute guy, but still). The single dad in *Pretty in Pink* who, again with daughter Molly Ringwald, supports all her dreams—even as he avoids going to job interviews, wastes his days away. And in Cameron Crowe's *Say Anything...*, John Mahoney plays the dad who puts his brilliant, kind, high school-superstar daughter first—even as he's ripping off his clients and ends up in jail. These fathers who really cared about their daughters in the teen movies of my adolescence were also depicted, at heart, as weak or broken men.

7. Whiskey Islands

DNA testing haunts me. I ran my own genes through the 23andMe test, then combed through the raw data looking for signifiers of alcoholism—not that I expected to find many. If there's an opposite to an alcoholic, I believe I am it.

Yet I have a counterintuitive theory: Anyone can get themselves a drinking problem. They just have to try hard enough. Genes have less to do with problem drinking than habit. Any of us can rewire our brains and our neurology to become addicted to a substance like cigarettes or heroin or corn syrup—and equally so to alcohol. Take smartphones. Take the internet. We didn't have them until about two seconds ago in human evolutionary terms, and now we can't get enough of them. We humans are easily addicted to myriad available temptations.

But genes of course play a role in why I am not a drinker. Part of it is my comical lack of tolerance, due in part to my bird-bone build. Half a beer in and my cheeks are pink. Two glasses of wine without a meal and I'm slurring my words. I'm very careful to eat the whole time I have a drink near me and to attack that drink in teeny tiny sips spread out over the longest possible amount of time. But I've known plenty of women with bonier builds than mine who can drink me under the table.

What specific genes are linked to alcoholism? The scientific jury is out; controversy reigns on the subject. But I'd found a list! I was going off some very cutting-edge data, compiled on A Random Website I Had Found. It listed dozens of genes supposedly linked to alcoholism. By whom, and to what degree—these were not addressed. Still, I searched gene after gene, and sure enough, I had none of these markers.

It's a mystery. How could my dad be a serious, old-school alcoholic—the deadliest kind of all—and yet I seem to have been spared those genes?

They are largely spelled out in his name: Neal MacLaren Harlan. I miss saying it, seeing it, hearing it. The poet in me loves the flowing resonance of those l's, r's, and n's, and the little lesson in our family tree, each name hailing from a different corner of Ireland, Scotland, and England. Or as I've come to call them, the Whiskey Islands.

Why are northern Europeans far too often binge-drinking drunks, while southern European people tend to drink in moderation? You know: the French or Italians or Spaniards who sip a glass or two of wine with a meal, and that's it, wine-wise that day, for them. Why, equally, are many Native American tribes so susceptible to alcoholism, but East Asian peoples—from whom native tribes long ago descend—are at far lesser rates?

A compelling theory holds that a tide of alcohol use has washed across different cultures at varying speeds over the millennia. The longer alcohol has been present in a culture, the higher its people's tolerance of it. So alcoholism rates are much lower in southern Europe, where wine has been produced since the Neolithic. But as you leave Rome or Madrid and head north and west to Dublin or Edinburgh, alcohol is an ever-more-recent arrival in those cultures, places, and peoples—and so more frequent the problem drinking.

I'm not sure I buy this theory entirely. But I've been to these cities, and it does help explain what evenings out on the town tend to look like.

8. Hungry Ghosts

Dr. Gabor Maté's *In the Realm of Hungry Ghosts* may well be the most scientifically rich, beautifully written, and flat-out helpful book on alcoholism and addiction. My dad was an alcoholic—those special, special people—but he was also a two-pack-a-day smoker. After he gave up drinking, he took up compulsive snacking. He and addictions kept finding each other.

Maté is a physician who has worked for decades with street addicts at a clinic in Vancouver, Canada. His book is rife with insights, but I'll highlight one of its most memorable arguments for me: That addiction cannot be explained by genes. While a genetic component exists, it is very minor compared to the effects of early nurturing—or lack thereof.

And we're talking *very* early nurturing. Extreme stress in vitro and in early infancy impacts human brain chemistry, including that shifting stew of available endorphins, serotonin, and dopamine, as well as the development of the prefrontal cortex (the brain's planning, discernment, and decision-making center). Imbalances and their discomforts created in the first months of life—whether through trauma, neglect, malnutrition, or other serious challenges—can create lasting imprints and deficiencies. These may explain a person's attraction to addictive substances in adolescence or adulthood.

Adopted identical twin studies have often been cited as clear evidence that alcoholism and "addictive personalities" are inherited traits. Two identical twins adopted by different families in infancy, who'd been born to a birth mother with a history of addiction, nearly always become addicts themselves—even when their adopted families have no addiction problems. Maté points out that in vitro stress hormones can impact neurology, that an addicted woman, or a woman partnered with an alcoholic or drug-addicted man (which raises her chances of being abused by a factor of thirteen), giving birth to twins and then handing them over to an adoption agency, can in itself explain lasting imbalances in brain chemistry.

For healing, Maté recommends a layered and lifelong approach to treatment, including therapy, support groups, psychopharmaceuticals, meditation, spiritual practices, and physical exercise. He actually ends his book with a point-by-point explanation for why AA's twelve-step program works.

Several years back I'd noticed a fresh crop of very loud anti-Alcoholics Anonymous evangelizers out there in the media, possibly trying to make professional names for themselves by Taking a Very Clear Stance against AA. Yet their critiques were nothing new, as I remember my parents calmly discussing and addressing all of these complaints eons ago in the Reagan years: that AA is a cult or too religious or blasphemous or dangerous because it's not run by mental healthcare professionals. AA was the original public, anonymous support group, and it's evolved into many local iterations over the years—some brilliant and useful, some less so.

I asked my mom about my dad's years with AA. How did it work for him? Here's how she explained it:

"The groups your dad went to, they weren't religious. The 'higher power' they talked to wasn't god-directed. A 'higher power' could be like a mantra—same principle. What you're saying is, I as an individual am not doing a good job controlling my drinking, so I need to stop trying to control it, and so I hand it over. *It's an emotional method of letting it go. And then making that moment last as long as possible.* You're letting it go to a higher power, meaning that I can't control this, but I can deal with it moment to moment to moment, and you make that moment last as long as you can, hopefully forever. You're meeting with people who want the same thing, and you support each other, and that really helps. It's astounding how well it works."

This method may not work for everyone, but it's worked for so many, including my dad. The help it offers may only be temporary. But so is everything.

9. Biofeedback

My dad had a twice-daily meditation practice during all those sober years: every morning, every night, for twenty-minute stints. I'd see him on the living room couch just sitting there, eyes closed, like he was cat-napping. But I could sense the subtler way my dad had exited the building: his imagination out in the sky, or maybe somewhere inward and quantum, but far away. He'd released himself from the worries and dramas of each day into a calming, freeing, disembodied distance.

It was, in the 1980s suburbs, pretty exotic stuff. He'd started his practice back when nobody other than committed, guru-seeking hippies were meditating (my dad, not a hippie, sported a "dry look" hairstyle and a near-continuous business casual look on the weekends). How he'd discovered meditation was through his study and practice of biofeedback.

Today, "biofeedback" has been rebranded as "neurofeed-back," perhaps to give it a newly relevant twenty-first-century spin, but it's the same thing: using one's conscious mind to access and control unconscious neurological and biological processes. My dad was really, really good at this.

He'd studied biofeedback because of his dental problems, which required painful root canal surgeries. My dad was worried that the stronger painkillers would remind him too much of being drunk, would endanger his sobriety. And so he taught himself to minimize the pain using only his mind, gleaning these techniques from books. The dental surgeon was so impressed, word of my dad's practice got him recruited into a biofeedback study at a local university.

My dad taught me his method, using the much-less-trying example of headaches: You picture where the headache is causing the pain, its exact location in your head. See it as a form, a shape, that you assign a color. Then visualize the color softening, fading out, like you are washing it away.

It takes, for me, about fifteen minutes to do this. It's not easy. It requires patience and concentration, qualities the headache has already weakened. But it works. As often as not, though, I skip it and take an ibuprofen, like everybody else.

But I rely on it to manage a different kind of pain: the rare fine piercings when I see, say, a woman my generation out with her dad, or sometimes when my son does any of the countless things my dad would have gotten such a kick out of—the little jokes, the drawings, all the music-playing, just himself being himself. *Dad, you're missing all of this!* The pain, colored like a bruise, stings my throat and chest. I breathe and try to fade it, pale it, into transparency, so that my real, non-wishful life can stand clear before me.

10. Talk About–able

Most deaths in the developed world are caused by sad, terrible, but talk about–able things: illnesses such as cancer or heart disease or wrenching sudden accidents. These causes of death possess no hint of culpability. No whisper of suicide casts any shade.

Alcoholism is an illness. Everyone says it; I'll bet few truly believe it. Drinking is viewed, in the end, as a choice, and so a moral issue. America is a puritanical nation at heart, but mostly because we humans are a puritanical species. We tend to prefer clear divisions of blame, order over nuance. A person with Crohn's disease may accidentally eat gluten pasta and find themselves in a hospital. But no alcoholic accidentally goes to a bar, accidentally orders a gin and tonic, and then accidentally drinks another seven. Right?

My dad, during those thirteen years of sobriety, was very clear about this: alcoholics know what's at stake, and when they drink, it's their choice.

So my dad must have chosen to die.

Or maybe he was wrong about how much choice he had, once he'd lost the grip on his life, was flooding his system daily with alcohol. Don't we all know that drinking severely impairs judgment, so that choices become blurred targets?

What I will never know: why he couldn't stop drinking, even after checking himself into those five different alcohol treatment centers. He refused to see me or my brother during those years, because he didn't want us to "see him like this." Or why we—my mom, my brother, and me, people he loved, helped, and was kind to, and who love him to this day—were not enough to keep him alive. Even though every alcoholic I've ever spoken to about this assures me that once an alcoholic is drinking, nothing can stop them but themselves. Right. Okay. But why didn't *he* stop himself?

People who have lost someone they love most in the world to either suicide or an "ambiguous death"—the quasi-suicide of "accidental" overdose, the slow suicide of alcoholism or drug addiction, jumping or possibly falling off bleachers to one's death, as was the case with my brilliant college poetry professor and mentor, take your tragic pick—are robbed of the simple, socially acceptable ability to say so.

"How'd you lose your father?"

"He had a heart condition" is what I've come up with. I picked "heart condition" for obvious symbolic reasons: viewed metaphorically, it's not a lie.

11. Dream City

I've had several uncanny dreams in my life. Sometimes—very rarely, but very precisely—I will dream a future or some facts I cannot possibly know. It's just intuition, the sixth sense with which our consciousness sometimes crosses paths, even as it tends to ignore our commands.

Here's an example of my dreaming the future. Well, not quite the future. It was more like the present, but far away.

It was February 14, 1997. My then-boyfriend and I were living in Manhattan's East Village, it was Friday night, and we'd had a truly wonderful Valentine's evening at a restaurant in our neighborhood. That night, I had a dream.

I dreamed I was in my favorite dream city—and as soon as I'd realized it, I cried out, "I'm back in my city!" Because I'd been there once before: A place part Manhattan, part Paris, part moonstone, part animal. Streets lifted like tendrils above parks and fountains; hills rose into sidewalk cafes. I'm walking down the street in front of West Village-style storefronts, and there, just strolling along in the crowd, I see him. "Dad!" I cry out, and he turns, and I run toward him, and we embrace. "I can't believe you're here!" I say. "Meg, I've missed you!" he says. We are so happy to see each other. Because, you see, it had been so long.

It had been, in real life, two years since he lost his health, his career, and started drinking. I hadn't seen him since he got into a cab in the West Village, after we'd had lunch, so he could go to the airport, make his way to Algeria. It was the last time I ever saw him.

But now: Here he is! My missing father, found and well, his funny, good-natured self. We walk down the street, find an outdoor cafe, seat ourselves, and enjoy the rest of the afternoon.

That's it. We hung out. It was his presence that made me happy, nothing particular, just us enjoying an afternoon on this earth.

12. Higher Power

The next morning I woke up in my real dream city, New York, and told my then-boyfriend about my dream: *Such a great dream! It was like he was with me!* About an hour later the phone rang and my mother was telling me my dad was dead. He died alone, in his Lake Tahoe house. My dread was complete, like a solved equation. Except the solution was zero: a nothing, an absence, held in a forever present tense. Over the years since, it's had a way of putting things in perspective: the only good to come out of this. I never cry now—not from sadness. I'm as broken as ever, as anyone. But I'm much lighter on my feet about it. Does this count as some sort of healing?

That week did not possess a sequence I recall. Time cohered as a round solid mass, see-through, hard and still as glass. I was outside myself; I could not move interiorly. The finality of going over that cliff face: He was gone. No more hope.

The only thing I remember from that week was going late one night to a diner on Avenue A. It was a completely average Greek New York diner, by which I mean, a perfect diner. I was with the man who is now my husband, now the wonderful dad to our son.

We walked in and the stereo was playing a song at high volume: "Hey Jude." The peaks and swoops of the melody, the word *better* being sung as four drumming syllables, surged through me. My dad's favorite Beatles song, my favorite Beatles song, written by Paul McCartney for a very young Julian Lennon, who'd just been abandoned by his father, a ballad for how to live despite everything. I felt like I was under a spotlight— not unusual when walking into a New York Greek diner late at night—but also like I had no skin, no membrane at all, I was just bones, blood, and the truth of this song.

I offer it here to my son. I can't explain tragedies. But I do know music.

WHAT IS VANISHING

> The past itself, as historical change continues to accelerate,
> has become the most surreal of subjects—making it
> possible . . . to see a new beauty in what is vanishing.
>
> —SUSAN SONTAG,
> "Melancholy Objects,"
> *On Photography*

1. Near Jubail

We're treasure-hunting again in the open desert of Saudi Arabia's Eastern Province. This being my family, the treasures we seek are nothing so obvious as jewels or money. What we are after is broken beyond repair, rare and often perplexing in origin, at once priceless and almost certainly unsellable. This combination of attributes is irresistible to my people.

All around us, sand dunes stretch through glass-crisp atmosphere to the horizon, free of towns and roads, trees and any other living, rooted thing. Look on a map, and it might appear we are in the middle of nowhere, though, of course, it won't be labeled like that since "nowhere" is not a location but rather a judgment of value, presumed to be so clear it doesn't even need naming. And it is always wrong.

My parents' friend, a petrochemical geologist and amateur archaeologist who works with my father, invites us on his many trips to this place, like the one today. He's re-created in our minds what vanished here many centuries earlier, an incense trade route. It once ribboned the Arabian Peninsula, connecting camel caravans southward to Oman, north to what was once Mesopotamia, to routes continuing westward to the Levant and Egypt, or heading east, overland into what are now the national borders of Iran and Afghanistan, India and China. He's taught us how to find its remains, a technique that requires no tools, no machines, only the sharp eye and long patience of a beachcomber.

The sand is pale as bone; any dead animal desiccates swiftly to bone; a bright bone glare sunburns us from the ground up. So we look for dark patches, any fleck of darkness on the ground. These could be pieces of glassware or pottery, or, if we're observant and lucky, a grouped or ring-like pattern, the sign of a long-ago fire pit. Because the sands shift with the winds, every time we return to this stretch of desert over many months, it looks different, recontoured by traveling dunes, and reveals new ancient things.

Like a tiny buoy drifting along the desert's rippled surface, a blackened half-circle catches my eye. I pick up a corroded coin and brush sand away from the sun-warmed remnants of a Roman face. We've already found a few of these silver coins; they might have been minted nearly anywhere the Roman Empire once existed. We will add it to our collection of treasures: Assyrian red pottery fired four thousand years ago; palm-sized stone loom weights pre-dating the Old Testament; glass sections of thousand-year-old Egyptian perfume bottles; lapis lazuli beads shaped like rigatoni and carved in Mesopotamia, back when that was a place; and—my favorite, simply for their looks—thick earthenware potsherds glazed deep teal hailing from medieval Iraq. We found those in a fire pit formation, the biggest shard about a foot long.

The geologist has taken many such artifacts to the British Museum for identification. He's given my parents mimeographed field guides to Aramaic and Akkadian script, to the crosshatch patterns of ancient pottery styles found on the peninsula dating from 5000 BCE onward. And so our outings have pieced together a world history lesson for me as tactile as it is fragmented, as international as it is pre-national, as commerce-based as it is priceless: a random, broken assortment of the ancient world's caravan-worthy treasures, plucked from the Saudi sands in the late 1970s by me, an American kid, and my family.

There I stand in my *Here Today Gone to Maui* T-shirt and white sun hat, staring at a coin someone lost two thousand years or so earlier. That person and I are linked, one hand holding the coin to the next, across a vertiginous span of time. It's a thought that keeps flashing inside me like a trick of light, a reflection off the atomized quartz landscape. Someone dropped a coin during the Roman Empire, and much of recorded history later it's picked up by a kid in sand-filled sneakers.

≡

Months pass before the geologist confides a secret to my parents. North of the incense route, he discovered two enormous jars, tall as he is, buried in the sand. They are in near-perfect condition, he says, but are too heavy to move, so he has buried them further, hoping that someday they and the site around them can be properly excavated. They are in an ideal environment to be preserved, in fact, lolling amid dunes, since archaeological pieces are often stored in fine sand. If, that is, the jars can survive two imminent threats.

The first: Saudi Arabia's most extremist mullahs and their followers, bent on destroying evidence of non-Islamic religious cultures within the kingdom for being infidel, whether Jewish, Christian, or any of the polytheistic faiths that once thrived across the peninsula. The geologist tells us about a recent case, the smashing to bits of some 2,500-year-old remains of a long-vanished Jewish settlement on the Arabian Gulf coastal island of Tarout, about thirty miles from where we are standing. Though the Saudi Arabian royal family has regularly supported archaeological excavations throughout the kingdom, news of the finds is suppressed from public release, lest they attract the angry attention of zealous Islamic fundamentalists. It's an example of the philosophical divide between the ruling Ibn Saud family and the Wahhabi Islamic leaders with whom they've had a complicated alliance since the country's inception as a modern theocracy.

The second threat: people just like us. More precisely, people that are us. And not just the people squirreling away Roman Empire coins into the pockets of their shorts. The geologist and my dad are employed by Bechtel Corporation, itself hired by the Saudi Arabian government in 1975 for what will be—to this day—the world's largest civil engineering project, the construction of the petrochemical metropolis of Jubail. One perpetual irony of the construction and engineering industries is that excavations for new building often reveal very old buildings right before threatening to destroy them. The geologist knows that Bechtel's Jubail project is helping to expose for the first time and also partially demolish some archaeological remains from what he believes are—and will indeed turn out to be—one of the ancient world's oldest and most sophisticated civilizations.

Granted, this is a culture few people alive today have heard of; it was legendary, oh, say, two thousand years ago. The Arabian coastal civilization of Dilmun was first cited in Sumerian texts circa 3200 BCE as an expansive seaside country of great wealth, advanced maritime trade, and artesian well-fed gardens, with urban centers dotting the northern and western Gulf region, including the earliest incarnation of Jubail. By 2100 BCE Dilmun is named as the garden paradise in which Gilgamesh searches for a plant that gives eternal life. Some archaeologists and historians believe the story of Eden—and other garden paradises featuring eternal life, a common theme in ancient Middle Eastern religious traditions—was based on a location in Dilmun.

As for the geologist's buried jars, they might have fallen off a camel however many centuries ago, or they might have been connected to the mythic culture of Gerrha. It is another long-lost civilization, right down there with Dilmun in obscurity, though once described by Greek geographer Strabo as the wealthiest place on earth. The Gerrhan capital of Thaj—a city filled with Greco architecture, exquisite goldwork, and remnants of the largest marketplace of the Gulf region, starting in the third century BCE—will, years later, be excavated several miles north of our incense route walks.

Yet it is not evident that the areas in and around Jubail constituted a nexus of built human culture for thousands of years. By 1978 virtually no visible ruins of these places remained. Jubail is described to the westerners moving there at the time as a sleepy fishing village whose main industry, besides fishing from traditional wooden dhows, is free-diving for pearls. Saudi Arabia itself occupies a curiously redacted space in world history, often in those years boiled down to a quick study of Muhammad, the development of Islam, and the oil industries.

But the "Saudi" I get to know on those walks—for that is what my family calls the country, as if we were on a familiar, first-name basis with it—contains a lightly buried history of human civilization's deep, wandering roots. It traverses well beyond any versions of the peninsula then propagated by the Saudi Arabian or American governments, beyond any Islamic fundamentalist propaganda or Western stereotype. It contains the archaeological objects I've come to see as crucial evidence for what is always missing from view, for what has almost been obliterated, for the way almost everything—but not *everything*—disappears. Up pop these objects out of "nowhere," and lost histories get rewritten right into our present day. How we value these histories depends on the degree to which we see all human beings as interconnected, even across extraordinary versatilities of place and time, and in ways we can always do more to imagine.

2. Foley Square

In October 1991 I'm twenty-one years old and working for Bechtel, really a construction development partnership called Bechtel–Park Tower Properties, in an office building at 52 Duane Street in Lower Manhattan. My father finagled me an interview for the position, assistant to the comptroller, and it's my first full-time job. I'm two months into living in New York, where I've moved to attend New York University's graduate program in creative writing. My workdays are filled with accounting spreadsheet programs in which, on the sly, I write the poems I'll bring to Jean Valentine's evening workshops.

Outside the tall windows of my boss's office where my desk is stationed, I have a view rare for this centuries-old, workaday part of Manhattan, a stone's throw from city hall. Just past tiny Elk Street, I look onto a vast empty lot and see daylight and bare ground. The foundation for a new building is being dug, already carved down about fifteen feet below street level by backhoes rumbling across the site where Duane Street ends at Broadway's streaming traffic.

Every day, my attention wanders further away from my work inputting accounts receivable. Alongside the construction workers and banana-yellow Cats, people with the neatly casual, unweathered look of graduate students fill the site in ever greater numbers, many of them female, in jeans and sneakers, holding fine tools or little notebooks. They are archaeologists hired to excavate the site.

I know this because word of the archaeological discovery during the building dig has traveled the streets, literally airborne: "old human remains." Rumors, speculations, and jokes about the remains circulate everywhere, while I'm buying falafel from the Palestinian street vendor or a bialy from the Hasidic morning bakery, while I'm standing along the site's chain link fence with the Wall Street guys, the lawyers, the Brooklyn administrators, the cops, and the scores of bike messengers, all hanging around on a break, chattering our curiosity and blarney. The bodies could be New Amsterdam–era Dutch people. The bodies are definitely Revolutionary War soldiers. The bodies might belong to Algonquian people from before the city was founded. And this wild theory: it's got the Mafia written all over it.

But in October the rumors end. During a press conference attended by Mayor David Dinkins at the site, the archaeologists announce they've uncovered part of an enormous cemetery for African slaves and free African people dating from the 1690s to the 1790s. Only a few maps from the Dutch and English colonial eras designated its existence. It's a place no one believed could have survived the centuries of building on top of it.

The discovery of the African Burial Ground will retell the history of slavery in America through New York City's buried past. It will forever change the record of how New Amsterdam

and old New York was built. The city's infrastructure and architecture, its docks and buildings and original roads—such as
Broadway and the Bowery—were constructed by African slaves.
Their remains bear witness to the manual labor that sometimes
literally broke their backs, to living conditions that resulted
in nearly half the remains belonging to children. Estimated to
contain between ten and twenty thousand graves, the cemetery
gives evidence that slavery in seventeenth- and eighteenth-
century New York City was as widespread and brutal as anything in the South.

But early news of the African Burial Ground's existence seems to meet with one overriding response in my
office: pity for the builders, tempered by sporting streaks of
schadenfreude.

"The GSA won't get their offices built any time soon," says
one guy I work with. "They're screwed." From him I learn a
few key things about our neighbors: The GSA is the General
Services Administration, and it's their new building that's
been halted indefinitely. The delay comes from federal law. If
construction of a government building reveals a historically
important site, contract archaeologists must be brought in to
excavate it before building can continue.

And I learn that my employer was similarly "screwed"—
at least in the view of my coworker—by the same law earlier in
the year. That's because Bechtel-Park Tower Properties is also
working on a GSA-funded project, the development of Manhattan's new federal courthouse at Foley Square, the city's largest
construction project in three decades. When completed, it will
be a lanky beauty as courthouses go, and later named for Daniel
P. Moynihan. But it's a project currently halted because of artifacts discovered at the site, an accidental find that will result in
the largest archaeological dig in New York City's history.

The courthouse site overlaps what was once Five Points, the notorious nineteenth-century slum. A few years later, Luc Sante's visceral history of Lower Manhattan, *Low Life*, will be released, and take its place forevermore on my short list of favorite books. About a decade later, Five Points will star as the setting for Martin Scorsese's movie *Gangs of New York*. But back then, all I know is that Five Points had been packed with poor, mostly Irish immigrants who'd fled the famine, none of whom had yet been played by Liam Neeson. The site encompasses two blocks between Pearl and Worth, where the early 1800s buildings and their privies and garbage pits were located, the latter considered treasure troves to archaeologists. The number of artifacts retrieved from these fourteen urban lots will be staggering: more than 850,000 objects.

Until that moment, I've barely given the courthouse site a thought, too dazzled by my sudden incarnation as a brand new New Yorker, graduate student, and working professional and by a logistical reality that involves hours each weekday of teetering at top speeds across cobblestones and subway stations in my sales-rack corporate outfits. Mostly, I am working hard to ignore how comically out of place I feel in my new job, one I'll manage to keep for another eight months.

That lunchtime I head two blocks east to the site, a wedge-shaped expanse that at first glance looks bombed out, cratered clean away. A few dozen thoughtful-faced people in jeans and sun hats, holding delicate instruments, and mostly covered with dirt—whom I now recognize as archaeologists—stand inside it, inspecting old stone walls or foundations two stories below street level. What had stood here most recently was a large parking lot. But instead of paving paradise, someone in the 1960s had put up a parking lot where tenements with names like "Gates of Hell" and "Brickbat Mansion" once stood.

Named for the five spokes created by the intersection of three streets—Anthony (today's Worth), Cross (now Park), and Orange (now Baxter)—Five Points was the most populous slum in American history, synonymous in newspaper reports in the nineteenth century with extreme poverty, brutal street crime, gangs, prostitution, outbreaks of cholera and tuberculosis, and the then-shocking fact that poor white immigrants speaking a foreign language—the Irish—lived, worked, and caroused alongside free black people (slavery was outlawed in New York in 1827). Later, when I learn all of this, I will realize that many of those African New Yorkers had family buried one or two generations earlier in the African Burial Ground. What they felt as buildings rose over their families' graves can only be guessed.

But that day, what I notice most about the site is its silence, as if this piece of the island had paused. Time seems to have stopped right there, on Worth Street in Foley Square, seems even to be turning, tunneling backward through the hush of buried facts, ones that will—like the African Burial Ground—change history. Time doesn't seem to do that very often, not in New York.

In the two months since I've moved to Manhattan, the city seems barely able to keep its past underground. It is apparently erupting on every street corner. But the coincidence of two major government-funded buildings going to ground the same year and amid the city's original streets—not to mention four blocks from each other—is unprecedented. Despite being the oldest major city in the United States, New York possesses the nation's worst record for historical preservation (at least according to a fascinating history of its archaeology, *Unearthing Gotham*). This aligns with the city's mythology: New York moves faster than anywhere. New Yorkers rush toward the nearest future, the next gig, deadline, deal. New Yorkers have no time to look back.

A minority of New Yorkers, though, just can't help looking back: its poets, its wanderers, its history lovers, the people who seek and find meaning in the past as if it were a form of spirituality. People, in other words, like me.

Yet I am also my father's daughter. I grew up in the large-scale construction and engineering industry. Most of us take for granted that, like any great city, New York is its buildings: the streets these buildings landmark, the shapes and textures they carve through the air, the shadows they cast like eccentrically timed sundials, the views they unfurl from top floors. By necessity, their builders—driven by budgets and deadlines, by staffs of engineers, architects, construction workers, accountants, and lawyers, each with conflicting mandates and priorities—aren't exactly the poets or philosophers of this world. They sometimes produce monstrosities that will then evolve before our eyes. For example, the Twin Towers were widely reviled when they went up in 1973, but during the nine years I lived in Manhattan, they seemed beloved for their flashy, five-block-high brawn. The old neighborhood will sometimes get razed. The new generation will move in and see it all differently, anyway.

Look closely, and a place toggles across time, all its presents and pasts. A place contains its strata of change, captured in situ, made seemingly solid. But it is barely more solid than its future. And that can be unnerving to notice.

Back near my office, the archaeologists' work never seems to cease. They work during rainstorms under clear plastic tents, where they sift pans of red dirt and inspect their finds. I see them at work after dark, illuminated by floodlights, when I leave the office late.

And discoveries from the African Burial Ground keep rising from the earth. Dozens of beads were found around a woman's skeleton, I hear one day. Those beads, her bones, the woman I imagine she was, appear in my mind every time I look out the office window. In the coming days, I hear more details about her: the almost disintegrated white fabric she'd been shrouded in, her head aligned to the rising sun according to the burial practice in her native West Africa, the number and quality of beads possibly signifying her role as a revered spiritual leader.

African culture, alongside European, forms the deepest substrata of the city of New York, its built urban landscape: this vast cemetery of its people, the alignment of their graves, containing the cowrie shells and blue beads they considered sacred, the buttons from Revolutionary War jackets, and the silver earrings they once wore. In Lower Manhattan in 1991, no visible landmarks from this original culture remain. It appears to be nowhere, until now.

3. Two Burial Grounds

Today, New York's African Burial Ground is a place, a memorial of sculpture and garden at the corner of Duane and Elk Streets and a national monument since it opened in 2007. Around the corner is an interpretive center dedicated in 2010 to the site's history and artifacts, tucked into the ground floor of the GSA administrative building at 290 Broadway, the one that did finally get built next to my old office on Duane Street. In 2013 I visit both places.

Among many other stories, the interpretive center details the controversies and travels of the site's human remains after the excavation I witnessed in the early 1990s. First, African American community members and politicians successfully lobbied to halt construction of a parking tower where the monument now stands. They then worked to transfer excavation of the site from the original contract archaeology firm to one experienced in African American burial grounds and to send the skeletal remains to a leading forensic anthropologist, Howard University's Michael Blakey, for study. But the various parties involved were divided for years over how the remains should be treated, whether as sacred objects, opportunities for historical research, or both. Finally, the groups agreed that further disturbance of the site's graves should cease and the 419 individuals already exhumed should be reburied, which they were in a large ceremony in 2003.

And so the monument reincarnates the African Burial Ground as a literal cemetery and an architectural memorial. Amid the site's grasses and trees stands an open-air court of polished granite spiraling just below street level and inscribed with languages, symbols, and maps from across the African diaspora. To the west rises a twenty-foot-high granite vestibule, a mirror image of the subterranean depth at which the graves were discovered. The remains of all 419 free and enslaved Africans originally buried here are reinterred within these grounds. Their descriptions—nameless, dateless epitaphs now taking place in history ("Burial 284 man between twenty and twenty-eight years")—are carved into the granite walls. The architect, Rodney Leon, has said he wants the sculpture to be walked through, touched, and experienced by everyone. As I move through it, the memorial feels like a fountain fed from great depths, its curving, reflective spaces mimicking water's undulating motion, primal force, and meditative pull. But it is the visitors who provide the movement, the force, the meditations; it is we who learn of and remember what it marks.

And the monument embodies this stark, uncanny fact: no object, no artifact, no matter how rare or extraordinary, can survive the tides of Manhattan and speak above them. In the language of New York, only a place can hold its own, can communicate the degree to which its subject counts, and is designated for permanence. Like nowhere else, New York is a city where the metaphors of location shape its mythology, a shared, tightly wired mythology of cross streets, parks, storefronts, and neighborhoods that elides with millions upon millions of private ones. At the most basic level, something is important in New York if it has its own address. The interpretive center, however thoughtfully curated its artifacts are, inhabits a space that looks as if it could be replaced with a future Starbucks. A memorial park crafted of black granite, sprawling over fifteen thousand square feet of prime Lower Manhattan real estate and shining with luxurious quantities of natural light changes the map. It speaks to the ages. It means business.

Place is an object of location and so always presumed to be discoverable. Objects in the usual sense have a way of being stolen, of getting crushed to bits, of going missing. In the short term, places so rarely do.

But sometimes they do. And in broad daylight.

In 1842 Charles Dickens was appalled when he took a tour of Five Points—for which he demanded police accompaniment—and famously reported of it: "All that is loathsome, drooping, and decayed is here." Dickens, though, was never a fan of its most populous inhabitants, the Irish, whom he'd once called a "racially repellent" people. Indeed, Five Points' infamy as the world's urban capital of crime, vice, and poverty supplied garish and exciting details for several of the era's most virulent biases: anti-immigrant, anti-black, anti-Irish, and anti-Catholic. Newspaper reports on Five Points throughout the nineteenth century trafficked in the shock and horror of its purported grotesqueries: gang wars, saloon brawls, and streetwalkers selling papers. And there was some truth to all of it.

The voluminous findings from the Five Points dig at Foley
Square in 1991 were studied by a team of archaeologists led by
Rebecca Yamin of John Milner Associates. Her group spent
years analyzing, cataloging, and photographing the more than
850,000 artifacts found in the site's privies dating to Five
Points' nineteenth-century heyday. They cross-referenced
building addresses with census, directory, and bank account
information to piece together a more complete portrait of the
neighborhood's inhabitants.

In 1997 Yamin sketched out her firm's unexpected findings
in an *Archaeology* magazine article, "New York's Mythic Slum:
Digging Lower Manhattan's Infamous Five Points." The surprise? Five Points was mostly filled with gainfully employed
people who saved their money, kept a nice table, and led conventional lives.

True, behind the basement brothel at 12 Baxter in the 1840s
were cast-off glass urinals made for women, once used by pros-
titutes bedridden with venereal disease.

But as hundreds of thousands of other artifacts bear witness,
most Five Points tenement dwellers worked long hours in regular if low-paying jobs to purchase the same quality items found
in middle-class households: ceramic tea ware and dinnerware
from Staffordshire, olive oil bottles imported from Lucca and
Marseille, Parisian perfume flasks, redware flowerpots, and the
trendy decorative figurines *du jour*, ceramic Staffordshire dog
heads. Five Points children owned marbles, dice, and teacups
inscribed with their first names, just like children from higher-
income enclaves.

Many of these humble objects might be found in somebody's
attic or an average antique store. They strike me, each individually, as not so remarkable, similar enough to some random household items that have survived from my own Amer-

ican family ancestry from the 1800s. What is extraordinary is
their sheer untouched quantity, their context of having been
in situ, right under the streets of Manhattan, where they'd carried on their lifeless existences in nearly the exact condition
as when they were discarded, like a sediment layer of the city's
nineteenth-century human culture.

After Yamin's group finished work, eighteen Five Points
pieces were exhibited in a small display at the South Street Sea-
port Museum. They are all that remain of the artifacts from the
Foley Square dig today.

The other 850,000-some objects were archived in the basement of Six World Trade Center. On September 11, 2001, when
the face of Tower 1 collapsed on top of that building, every one
of the artifacts was destroyed.

A footnote amid the whole-scale mass murder and monumen-
tal wreckage surrounding them, their loss is one I learned of
while reading the *New York Times* two months after 9/11, on the
other side of the country, no longer a New Yorker by about a year.

Rebecca Yamin will be later quoted in *Archaeology* magazine: "It's hard to get emotional about the artifacts; they're just
not significant compared to the loss of human life."

Artifacts are not significant at all compared to human life.
Yet they are significant enough to halt major construction jobs,
to spend careers studying, and to rewrite histories of entire
places and cultures. Those 850,000 artifacts went fairly rap-
idly from being historically significant objects no one knew still
existed to objects that no longer exist, whose significance is
diminished to almost zero within the context of their loss.

But not zero. Not quite.

Almost everything—but not *everything*—disappeared.

And their story connects the unlikely crosscuts of accident,
history, and place so common in archaeology.

The Five Points artifacts—decades worth of junk to their mostly Irish Famine-era owners—survived beyond their burial in privies, after their chance discovery during a massive building dig. Their history was reclaimed after painstaking archaeological work in the twentieth century. Nearly all these objects were destroyed when the Twin Towers fell, at the hands of the terrorist hijackers of two airplanes, who hailed, but for one, from the Arabian Peninsula.

4. Tupperware

After my family collected the artifacts from the vanished incense route, we took them out of Saudi Arabia when we moved away in 1979. Along with their geologist friend, my parents believed we were preserving the objects from obscurity, radical Islamic fundamentalists, or their most likely fate, being destroyed by the construction crews that would over the coming decades develop the incense route area into what is today the largest industrial city in the Middle East. I know the artifacts do not belong to me. Yet I'm the one who has kept them.

I hold my favorite shard, hailing from Iraq around 1,200 years ago, a chunk of an earthenware pot's circular base about the area of my splayed hand and standing four jagged inches tall. Teal glaze streaked with cobalt sheathes the exterior, as smooth to the touch as enamel. In its present day, the shard belonged to somebody's pot for storing food, an ordinary domestic item. But in my hands, across the intervening span of centuries, its original world signals from a great distance, as if in a root language. It's a world where blue-green pottery transmits a beauty I understand, the color of garden paradise transported into a future I inhabit.

I don't hold the shard very often. It's usually wrapped up—along with my other artifacts—in the original canary yellow paper towels my mother used in our Jubail kitchen back in the 1970s, their brown-and-orange floriated patterns still crisp, all tucked into two small Tupperware boxes of similar vintage. Now even the Tupperware and paper towels feel archaeological to me, exotic artifacts of middle-class Americana circa 1979.

My mother has the best incense route pieces locked away in a storage unit; I haven't seen them in decades. The rest of my collection comprises a mix of real, guessed, and unknown objects annotated by her, including five stone loom weights with eraser head–sized holes, alongside the handwritten note, "2,000 years old (older?)"; a dozen potsherds of black chlorite, the material favored by Eastern Province pot-makers four thousand years ago; and the delicate base and neck of a green glass amphora, for which I have another handwritten note from my then-thirty-nine-year-old mom: "1,000 years old, Egyptian (good condition—rare!)."

In 2013 the Saudi government launched an unprecedented museum exhibition of the kingdom's archaeology, *Roads of Arabia*. Featuring the hundred-thousand-year-long human record on the Arabian Peninsula and co-funded by Saudi Aramco (the Saudi Arabian Oil Company, in business since 1933), the showing opened at the Louvre in Paris and traveled to several museums around the Western world, including San Francisco's Asian Art Museum, where I saw it in January 2015.

My Tupperware-stored shards are—to a precise degree that startled me—like the reject versions of several pieces in that exhibition: loom weights and black chlorite pots pre-dating the Egyptian pyramids, multicolored medieval Egyptian glassware, and a pieced-together, three-foot-high Iraqi jar circa 600–800 CE—the same beautiful teal-glazed earthenware as my favorite potsherd.

Thus Saudi Arabia's deep history has been introduced to the world stage in one recent fell swoop. What could explain this about-face by the Saudi government, this very public airing of the true complexity of Arabian cultural and religious history, one not limited to the Wahhabi interpretation of Islam? The most obvious, cynical, and likely explanation: its government is engaging in a little PR. Since September 11, 2001, of course, Saudi Arabia represents to the West a different place than the distant, deliriously oil-rich desert lands of my childhood, now infamous as the home country of Osama bin Laden and fifteen of the nineteen hijackers. How Saudi Arabia leaped up out of "nowhere" to produce so many key players in anti-Western terrorism has never been answered.

We designate "nowhere" at the risk of many kinds of ignorances, and sometimes at our peril. But in my idiosyncratic eye-witnessing of building and archaeology in New York and Saudi Arabia, the history of every place contains a fluid, shape-shifting force. The truth of the past reveals ongoing discoveries rather than any completion.

If nothing else, archaeology saves us from the witlessness of certainty: If history ever seems written in stone, then it's time to find some more stones. And there will always be more stones. This view of history includes our own. Our pasts are never fixed, at least not as we've experienced them, because there is always more to our stories, even if only by searching for it.

When considering artifacts of whatever origin, some questions will dog us: What do we owe to the past? How much of it should we dredge up, how do we use it, and where do we put it? These are ideas we may pick at regarding our own family histories, the stories and belongings that haunt us. Artifacts, somewhat ironically, let in fresh air, opening these questions to a vantage point beyond the personal, beyond the limited range of notes carried by any single human voice. They grant hard evidences of other lives fully lived, cultures fully formed, about which we may know almost or exactly nothing, yet which existed as surely as our own. They transcend our need or reasons for them.

We could crush them into dust, sure. They are, after all, only objects. But they can also survive beyond ourselves and so connect our experiences of them within a human continuum of cultural exchanges across time and space. We can try to understand each other—even others long dead—across impossible distances this way. We can peer at some artifact up close, be drawn into its original provenance going back dozens, hundreds of generations. That closeness and that distance create its own relationship. We stand in someone's never-to-be-experienced future, peering at their broken pot. It is touching, yes, that word—but what is it touching and with what is it doing the touching? Our senses of scale and depth, of intimacy and eternity, feel tapped and flexed all at once. Artifacts help us see the whole shape, the real expanse of the human race, our habitation. Even if we individually scatter and dissipate, atomized as sand.

Some things will remain. We can never guess what.

SETTING STONEHENGE

The medium is the message.

—MARSHALL MCLUHAN,
Understanding Media

1. Nimoy (5:50 a.m.)

It's a cloudy August morning just after sunrise, and my family
and I are speeding about a hundred miles west of London in our
rental car, bisecting the Salisbury Plain on the A303. Giant figures the color and heft of elephants appear on a treeless green
hill, and an instant snaps before I recognize what they are.
"Stonehenge! Hey, is that Stonehenge?" my son asks, my partner swerves as he takes a look, and I answer with a choked-up
"Yes!" Latent emotions flood my system with embarrassing
force, like I've run into a love-defining first crush.

The big stones are gathered in a circle as if around a water-
ing hole, a campfire, some leaning into each other, others toppled over like they've had a few too many. I'm seeing them for
the first time in person, and their jagged outline seems both
familiar as my own hands and mildly hallucinated, as if the site

had appeared from a distant universe made suddenly material—a fragment of a five-thousand-year-old world.

Who built Stonehenge, how did they do it, and why? As a kid, I'd adored Stonehenge for these unsolved mysteries that had cleverly perplexed adults for so long, as if it were a benevolent entity visiting us continuously from the deep human past, wishing we could understand its heavyweight, three-dimensional language. I'd absorbed as revolutionary fact the beloved shlock 1970s TV documentary show, *In Search Of... The Magic of Stonehenge*, in which host Leonard Nimoy reported that the site was built as a mystical astronomical clock, whose time we could now tell using the most cutting-edge, van-sized computers. (The results, I'm sorry to note, were a little off—but more on that later.)

Like a powerful magnet, Stonehenge has long attracted alluring, brilliant, and whack-job theories. It pre-dates the Egyptian pyramids by five centuries and holds the lead for mystery: No indigenous written language—hieroglyphic or otherwise—remains to explain any of it. In lieu of scriptural clues or contemporaneous accounts, the site has inspired all manner of legend, science, technological innovation, spirituality, astronomical measurement, projection, mythology, and abject nonsense to explain it, rising like so many scaffoldings visible only to the believers.

True to form, I'd made my family awaken before dawn to visit the place because of my own pet interests. I am fascinated by prehistory, for exactly the reason I am weary of my smartphone. I've visited dozens of Neolithic sites across the British Isles, for the same reason I'm bored of addictive internet searches. I am no Luddite, nor do I yearn to wear rawhide, live in a cave, or lack decent dental care. But I wonder: What is the cost of digital technologies meant to save us time—but often so distractingly waste it? What of ourselves do we lose to "smart" devices, to this Silicon Age where artificial intelligences often rush in before our natural ones?

We don't say anyone came from a primitive society anymore; we say they had primitive *technologies*. But these simpler technologies may have engaged all the genius, complexity, and insight human beings can muster. If the medium is the message, then Stonehenge's built landscape—one requiring an estimated *ten million* work hours to construct—telegraphs at the least A Major Belief System capable of directing such extraordinary creative labor. What can we discern of this belief system from recent large-scale excavations at the site? Could it enrich or illuminate our lives now?

And so, as my family drives into the Stonehenge Parking Lot, I search my smartphone for the email with our ticket number to enter one of the oldest buildings still standing on the planet.

2. Target (6:05 a.m.)

Our time to visit Stonehenge begins at 6:15 a.m. and lasts for one hour. Months earlier I'd made arrangements for this "Stone Circle Access"—time-slots limited to thirty visitors that get you close enough to touch the stones (though touching them is a no-no) and held in the early morning or late evening. If you show up during normal visiting hours, you can only view Stonehenge from behind a fence—like the stones are zoo animals kept in their own special habitat.

We park and head toward the small crowd waiting by a shuttle bus outside the gleaming visitor center. The stones are nowhere within view, tucked far enough behind a long-sloping hill due east to justify the shuttle bus. And I've realized the hot competitive logistics required of our next several minutes.

Because here's the silly yet pressing concern of going to

Stonehenge with your kid: you might want a photo of your child standing among the stones like you just stumbled upon the place, magically free of anyone else milling around.

In order to do this, you must be willing to race the other visitors to reach the site first.

I whisper my plan to my family, and my son nods and assumes a poker face. We loiter by the reproduction Neolithic house, while everyone else files on to the shuttle. Then I make sure we are the last to hop on, so that—in what comprises the entirety of my cunning plan—we will be first off.

The shuttle sweeps us over the mile-and-a-half hill line, and I get the sensation of time-traveling in place, as if we are now entering 3000 BCE in our climate-controlled pod. Shafts of sunlight break through clouds over the Salisbury Plain—which once qualified as a sort of prehistoric New York Greater Metropolitan Area, its yellow-green landscape studded with thousands of Neolithic and Bronze Age sites including standing stones, burial mounds, and hundreds of houses.

When the shuttle stops, my son and I leap out, gape at the Stonehenge skyline rising ahead of us, and shoot down the path toward it. I assume we're in the clear, only to realize we are speed-walk racing five Nordic-looking women. But as long-distance fast-walking is my most semi-exceptional quasi-athletic talent, and with my kid jogging alongside me, we keep our small lead.

Picture Stonehenge's layout like a huge target composed of nine concentric rings of earthworks, holes, or stones, all stretching more than three hundred feet in diameter. My son and I reach the first ring and outer perimeter, or "henge"—the term for the bank and ditch enclosures that ring Neolithic stone circles across the British Isles. Its twenty-feet-wide impression is still visible and marks the first stage of Stonehenge's millennia-long construction around 3100 BCE.

We then trot past the next three rings, all virtually invisible and grass-covered today. First we cross the circle of Aubrey holes, dating to Stonehenge's most ancient original structure: fifty-six evenly spaced depressions that once held standing Welsh bluestones weighing two or three tons apiece—and, as a painstaking forensic study revealed in 2016, the cremated remains of dozens of Neolithic women, men, and children. We bound another sixty feet and pass the so-called Y Holes and, several yards in, the Z Holes: two concentric rings that once held those same Welsh bluestones several centuries later, megaliths that were finally relocated to the inner circle about 4,200 years ago.

We barely beat the Nordic-looking women to the Stone Circle, where the remaining stones of the site's five inner rings lay in a hundred-foot-wide jumble. My kid stands along the northern stretch, smiles, and I manage to get a single shot of him as if we'd rented the place for ourselves, had splashed out on all thirty spots.

Then the five women dash into my camera's view from the right and toward the bulls-eye center of Stonehenge—the horseshoe formations of massive sandstones and smaller Welsh bluestones. They form a circle, link hands, and blast away the early morning silence.

3. Stone Circle (6:25 a.m.)

In piercing, high-pitched harmony, the women are choral singing at the top of their lungs. The song sounds medieval to me, à la Hildegard of Bingen, a lilting if high-volume polyphony.

I'm delighted by the beauty of their singing, curious why they chose this piece but just as interested to notice how carefully the other visitors, now filtering into the Stone Circle, pretend the singing isn't happening. We are all apparently the kind of people to have studied the Stonehenge website's instructions to visitors—"please respect each other's time inside the Stone Circle"—and realize this is our first test. The site's guidelines allow us to enact our own private Stonehenges through dancing, costumes, drumming circles, yoga, or whatever self-expressive means we desire—but not to query or otherwise pester anyone else about theirs.

My nine-year-old son—the only child there—is staring at the singers open-mouthed. We watch as they drop hands; their song dissolves like fog into the bright air.

Now I'm left to make sense of the Stone Circle, enough to point out the five rings to my kid: the massive sandstone sarsens forming the outer circle; inside that, a ring of smaller Welsh bluestones; next, the filled-in holes of the itinerant bluestones, where they'd once formed a double circle; and in the center area, two interlocking horseshoe formations, one of giant sarsens and the other, at Stonehenge's very heart, of bluestones.

But what I *see* are seventy-seven standing stones strewn higgledy-piggledy around us. From a distance and on maps, the site looks a lot more cohesive than when you're in the middle of it. I keep turning around, trying to absorb the broken-down layout, while my first impressions of Stonehenge come in a rush.

I'm struck by how truly enormous the sarsens are—looming as tall as thirty feet, a good six or seven feet wide and deep, weighing as much as sixty tons. Honed of pale gray sandstone quarried about twenty miles away at Marlborough Downs during the Bronze Age, only twenty-five of them are still upright; the other twenty lay on their sides. All are proportioned like blocks to be carved with the statues of giants.

Over the years, I've sometimes heard it claimed that Stonehenge is disappointingly small. I now wonder if these claimants have gotten anywhere near the stones or just sped past the site on the A303, where Stonehenge does appear on the small side since it sits *at a pretty good distance from the road*. Because when you're standing, dwarfed, beside them, the sarsens appear huge, absolutely massive, or as my son put it, "ginormous."

My eye keeps getting drawn to the sarsen circle's most finished section: the smooth unbroken line of four sarsens capped with lintels, like three linked doorways open to the Wiltshire hills (when the circle was intact, thirty sarsens once stood, forming thirty such "doorways"). And in the site's center, the three standalone trilithons—each composed of two extra-large sarsens capped by a single lintel—resemble very tall pi symbols.

I force myself to notice the diminutive bluestones, often no more than five feet high. Yet they are Stonehenge's show-stealing stars, boasting far more interesting histories: eighty or so bluestones were once dragged or possibly rafted via sea and rivers some 180 miles away in the Preseli Hills of southwest Wales. This long-haul travel happened during the New Stone Age, which, when you remember nobody had any metal implements or even wheels to aid them, makes Pembrokeshire seem like it might as well have been Neptune.

But my most overwhelming first impression is that I'm standing in a phenomenal theater-in-the-round: an open-air gathering and performance space in which we visitors—outfitted in our waterproof jackets and comfy shoes—are, right now, the very fortunate actors.

4. Calendar (6:30 a.m.)

I point to Stonehenge's most famous solar alignment. "That's the Heel Stone, lined up exactly where the winter solstice sun sets every year," I say to my kid, as we gaze at the standing stone just outside the henge's northeast perimeter.

We head to the Heel Stone and turn to face the Stone Circle. I explain how, if we were there on a clear December 21, the setting sun would illuminate one of sarsen circle's three doorways—its thirty-foot-high threshold blazing with orange light.

I'd already shared that Stonehenge may have been built as a three-dimensional astronomical clock—a solar, lunar, and stellar timekeeper. A beautiful old word describes such a thing: orrery, a sort of sundial writ large, keeping track of all the sky's cyclical occurrences. This theory is what fascinated me at his age: that Stonehenge was built to *interact* with both the sky and with time itself, framing and marking, reflecting and highlighting all celestial events, from moon risings to eclipses, as they marked the days, months, seasons, and centuries.

And the person most famous for trying to prove this theory was featured on my long-ago, beloved *In Search Of . . . The Magic of Stonehenge*: Dr. Gerald S. Hawkins, an astronomy professor at Harvard, Boston University, and the Smithsonian Observatory in the 1960s, who fed detailed measurements of Stonehenge's architectural layout along with historical astronomical data into an enormous computer, the Harvard-Smithsonian IBM 704. He concluded from this first-of-its-kind study that Stonehenge was itself a "Neolithic computer" that predicted astronomical events, findings he published in his best-selling 1965 book, *Stonehenge Decoded*.

Unfortunately, much of the data Hawkins fed into that shiny IBM was wrong. Just by using then-accepted archaeology, he assumed Stonehenge's construction began in 1900 BCE, and a good twelve hundred years *later* than its true groundbreaking around 3100 BCE—an error that throws off architectural correlations with some concurrent celestial movements. His key and very ingenious theory, meanwhile, was that the fifty-six Aubrey holes were used to track moonrises and lunar eclipses with the aid of two rotating wooden markers. But only from the site's recent excavations have we learned that those holes were dug to hold bluestones, along with cremated human remains—and so were used, in other words, as burial sites.

Gerald Hawkins is far from the only Very Serious Person to have had his scientific study of Stonehenge upended by the finer technologies of future scientists. Most notable is William Stukeley, born 1687, the Cambridge-educated antiquarian, physician, clergyman, and composer who is credited with no less than inventing archaeology as a field of study. While excavating Stonehenge, Stukeley noticed that the summer solstice sun rose *fairly* closely over the Heel Stone. He assumed this sun-drenched event on the longest day of the year must have held profound spiritual meaning for Stonehenge's builders—whom he decided were most likely Druids. News of Stukeley's conclusions fascinated the public, who have been showing up at Stonehenge for the summer solstice sunrise ever since—often by the thousands, and sometimes wearing Druid robes. The trouble is, the Druids did not build any phase of Stonehenge (their people, the Iron Age Celts, arrived in the British Isles far too late to take credit, around 300 BCE). And twenty-first-century archaeological work indicates that Stonehenge was not aligned in particular to the midsummer day, but rather to its midwinter corollary.

But other astronomical alignments at Stonehenge *have* held up. I point to one of the two remaining Station Stones located just inside the henge's perimeter—they once numbered four, forming a rectangle that framed the Stone Circle. "That stone marks the major moonset to the north," I say. "And a missing stone over there marks the major moonrise to the south. We don't know why, but they do."

"Cool," my kid says. Then he whispers, "Why are those people bending over?"

5. Alignment (6:35 a.m.)

"Those people" are a couple I will silently dub the Beautiful Crunchies: a young man and woman, both sporting long flowing hair and natural fiber exercise wear, who will spend the hour striking yoga poses among the stones. I will keep finding one or the other of them tree posing next to a sarsen or, eyes closed, deep in lotus near a trilithon. But right now they have positioned themselves along the Heel Stone's alignment with the Stone Circle to do sun salutations.

"Yoga," I say.

"Oh, yeah," he says. "You do that." Then: "Why?"

"I'm guessing they believe Stonehenge is a spiritual site, and that doing yoga here will be a meaningful experience—like they're tapping into the energy of the place."

He shrugs. "That's weird, right?" he asks.

"Well, no weirder than singing," I say. "There's a funny old idea," I continue, moving on to less firm ground, "where some people think invisible lines of powerful, healing energy run across the landscape—all across the world. They're called ley-lines, and they're not actually real," I say. "But people who believe in ley-lines think Stonehenge is a magical center for them."

My son looks around at the stones with a newly assessing, respectful eye. For a second, I do too. It's fun to think magic might exist as a form of nature we don't yet understand.

Ley-lines hit their stride as a cultural phenomenon in the 1960s—itself a sexy, peak news-making decade for Stonehenge. Another serious academic who gave the site worldwide attention in those years was Oxford University engineering professor Alexander Thom. His 1967 book, *Megalithic Sites in Britain*, introduced the concept of the megalithic yard—a unit of measurement, 2.72 yards to be exact, that Thom claimed, after measuring hundreds of ancient sites across the British Isles and Brittany, was universal to Stone Age megalithic architecture of Atlantic Europe. This suggested a cohesively developed Neolithic culture and regular peaceful contact among widely dispersed groups. But the megalithic yard, somewhat unfortunately for Thom and his measurement being taken seriously, was embraced by ley-line enthusiasts, who themselves tend to Venn-diagram neatly with neo-Druids, who in turn often annoy archaeologists by claiming Stonehenge as their ancestral burial ground and demanding that it be left alone. Alexander Thom did not believe in ley-lines, yet his name and his megalithic yard have been wound up with them ever since.

After the 1960s, no excavations of Stonehenge—or other organized on-site studies—were allowed until the twenty-first century. Luckily, in the past fifteen years (as I write this in 2018), new leadership at English Heritage, the government trust that controls Stonehenge and many prehistoric sites around it, has allowed three major digs.

The year 2003 marked the start of the largest excavation in Stonehenge's history: the five-year Riverside Project. Its lead archaeologist, Michael Parker Pearson, has written fascinating books on his findings, which—in the smallest of nutshells—boils down to this: Pearson believes Stonehenge was a monument created to unite Neolithic Britons, involving as much as *one-quarter* of the island's population during the peak years of its construction—a kind of rural American barn-raising party writ monumentally large. And that Stonehenge, once built, functioned primarily as a memorial to their ancestors, both as a cemetery and a temple to the dead.

Then, in 2008, English archaeologists Timothy Darvill and Geoff Wainwright excavated the Stone Circle for clues about the origins and uses of the bluestones. They were later able to locate the stones' source in western Wales's Preseli Hills—where bluestone circles much older than Stonehenge still stand, and where some local people believe the bluestone hills and the springs rising from them possess healing powers. Darvill and Wainwright concluded that the bluestones were relocated to Stonehenge for their associated curative properties, where they were used to construct Stonehenge as a center of healing—a sort of Neolithic Lourdes. The number of nearby ancient tombs containing the remains of seriously injured people who hailed from far away—the Amesbury Archer being the most famous example, a man born in the Alps during the Bronze Age—lends support to their theory.

Finally, since 2010, the massive Stonehenge Hidden Landscapes Project has surveyed the areas surrounding Stonehenge for prehistoric sites, including the largest dig in England's history, Durrington Walls—work that continues to this day.

And all three archaeological projects provide fascinating evidence that two different cultures—using different technologies and hailing from two genetically distinct peoples—built Stonehenge over a thousand-year span, possibly for several overlapping purposes.

6. Construction (6:45 a.m.)

My son now really wants to touch a sarsen, and I don't blame him. Though the site's guidelines are explicit, I ask one of the two guards standing, poker-faced, near us: "Excuse me, but I'm wondering: we're *really* not supposed to the touch the stones?" He grimaces a brief, somehow sympathetic nod of confirmation, then says, "Let me show you something."

The guard leads my family over to a sarsen, where he points out the word WREN inscribed faintly on its face. "Wow," I say, and share that just the day before in London, we'd seen Christopher Wren's masterpiece, Saint Paul's Cathedral.

"It's a beautiful place," the guard affirms. "But how would Wren have liked it if someone wrote graffiti on *his* building?"

I nod, keeping to myself how charming I find this graffiti—because Christopher Wren is the greatest English architect many of us might name, his four-hundred-year-old defacement of a sarsen seems basically acceptable to me. But I suppose if you're a guard at Stonehenge, you don't want anyone getting any funny ideas along those lines. First Wren; then who?

The guard and my partner launch into a spirited discussion about the construction of the sarsen circle and trilithons. My son, excited, joins in. The guard tells us about the successful experiments to replicate the raising of these giant stones involving deep pits, enormous wooden platforms, and a tip-and-lift, shove-and-heave methodology. They all three start shuffling around, lifting their arms to mimic lifting the stones—a pantomime probably done for centuries in honor of this bunch of hewn rocks.

I went to the Egyptian pyramids at Giza when I was about my son's age, and remember a similar conversation and pantomime involving my dad about how the colossal stones were put in place using scaffolding, ramps, and a lot of slave labor. At the time, I was totally convinced that this could be done—because, after all, clearly it *had* been.

The guard points to a lintel, or crosspiece, capping two uprights in the sarsen circle. "They carved the sarsens as if they were wood," he says. Specifically, they used the mortise-and-tenon system of woodworking: each lintel features two holes, or mortises, centered along the bottom at either edge, which fit perfectly into the little knobs, or tenons, jutting up from the top of each sarsen. So for some reason, the sarsens were fitted together using methods of *carpentry*.

As for transporting the sarsens from their source at Marlborough Downs nineteen miles away, modern reenactments employing a single thirty-ton stone, huge log sleds, ropes, and about two hundred people working twelve days straight have done the job. Meanwhile, experiments to replicate loading the Welsh bluestones onto boats and rafting them over long distances—from coastal western Wales to Bristol, then via rivers to Stonehenge—have utterly failed: the three-ton stones sink. The bluestones again prove more mysterious than the flashier, more photogenic sarsens.

But the Stonehenge Riverside Project also revealed much more accurate dates for the phases of the site's construction, which in turn shed new light on the people responsible for them.

Stonehenge was originally built by Stone Age people: Neolithic farmers who broke ground at the site around 3100 BCE. They brought the bluestones from western Wales—where they themselves may have originated—and used the silver-blue megaliths to construct Stonehenge's earliest stone circle in the fifty-six Aubrey holes. Inside those holes they'd first placed cremated human remains.

Then, over the next five or six centuries, this ethnic group disappeared—replaced by a genetically distinct people known as the Bronze Age Celts. Since no signs of battle are found in the archaeological record, the bluestone builders may have been decimated by plague or other disease brought by the later-arriving Europeans.

These Bronze Age Celts are responsible for building the sarsen circle and the massive sarsen trilithons around 2600 BCE. They not only kept the bluestones but moved them ever closer to the heart of the site, suggesting that these people understood and respected their ancient symbolism.

And new studies published in *Smithsonian Magazine*, *BBC News*, and elsewhere suggest that at least one of the bluestones' uses was making music.

7. Choir (7 a.m.)

My son is standing next to a bluestone, his ear barely an inch from it. He calls to me, eyes wide, "Mommy! The stone is making sound!"

I join him, listen close—and too hear a very faint ringing, like an echo or some auditory effect created by the wind blowing against its surface.

This observation has been made before. Local boy Thomas Hardy—who immortalized the stones in a dramatic final scene of his 1892 novel, *Tess of the D'Urbervilles*—once stated in an interview, "If a gale of wind is blowing, the strange musical hum emitted by Stonehenge can never be forgotten."

Stonehenge's possible acoustic properties have inspired a lyrical theory: that the bluestones were relocated from Wales because they can be played as musical instruments. If you smack a sandstone sarsen with a stick, it sounds like a dull thud. But do the same to a bluestone, and it emits a clear, low ringing that can heard as far as a half-mile away. Rocks used as bells are called lithophones, and bluestones have indeed been used as church bells in Wales for many centuries. Study of megalithic sites for such effects have spawned a new field of prehistoric study: archaeo-acoustics.

And an old name for Stonehenge, Côr Gawr, may provide another clue. Among local people and through the nineteenth century, Stonehenge was often called Côr Gawr (or, spelling-

wise, any combination of Côr or Choir with Gaur or Gawr). I
first ran across the term in Ralph Waldo Emerson's account
of his 1848 visit to Stonehenge, in which Emerson notes,
"Choir Gaur, or Côr Gawr, meaning Giant's circle or temple,
is only a British name for Stonehenge." By "British," Emerson
meant the Gaelic-speaking people living in Britain before the
Anglo-Saxons began colonizing the island in the fifth century,
the latter dubbing the place "Stonehenge."

How ancient a term is "Côr Gawr"? In modern Welsh,
gawr means "giant," while *côr* translates to "choir." Gaelic
languages like Welsh date at least to the Iron Age Celts, who
started arriving in the British Isles from Gaul around 300
BCE—bringing the culture we've long associated with all things
Celtic.

But linguistic researchers such as Peter Forster of Cambridge University and Alfred Toth of University of Zurich
believe the much older Bronze Age Celts spoke a root form of
the Gaelic language family called "proto-Celtic," which they
may have brought to the British Isles as early as 3100 BCE. Could
the name "Côr Gawr" date that far back? We'll probably never
know if these words survived so many centuries as some place-
names have, broken or corrupted but still identifiable, like fragments of ancient pottery or bone.

8. Myth (7:05 a.m.)

Until the last century, the most popular Stonehenge origin
story was that Druids had built it. Archaeologists today are
absolutely clear on the subject: Druids did not build Stonehenge. These mysterious religious figures arrived in Britain
a good two thousand years too late to take credit—as the lat-

est carbon-dating, forensic anthropology, and genetic testing methods have proven.

Druidism was the religion of the Iron Age Celts—those Gaelic-speaking tribes, dubbed Gauls by the Romans, who arrived in Britain around 300 BCE. Inconveniently for historians, Druids, though literate, maintained an oral tradition for their own cultural heritage, so what we know about their beliefs and practices comes from outsider sources—and for the most part their mortal enemies, the Romans. Classical writers such as Julius Caesar and Pliny the Elder claimed that Druids were priests and priestesses who worshiped nature, holding secret ceremonies in sacred groves; they were the "learned class" of the Celts; and they engaged in the occasional, blood-drenched human sacrifice.

So why are Druids so strongly associated with Stonehenge? Because the site's early archaeologists of the seventeenth and eighteenth centuries, including William Stukeley and John Aubrey (for whom the ring of stone-holes is named), made the educated guess that Druids must have built the place, since their Celtic tribes were, at that time, the earliest known inhabitants of Britain.

The idea stuck. And it captured the public's imagination, lending Stonehenge the romance of an ancient, exotic spirituality based on poetic language, magical rituals, and the natural alignments of seasons and astronomy. All of this helped fuel the Celtic Revival that would spread to Ireland, Scotland, and Wales, lasting well into the nineteenth century.

But when my family walks over to the mattress-sized slab called the Slaughter Stone—thus dubbed for supposedly being the site of human sacrifices, officiated by white-robed Druids—I have to explain to my son that no, nobody was ever slaughtered here. Archaeologists have found nothing to indicate a crime scene.

"So why's it called a Slaughter Stone?" he asks.

"People have active imaginations," I say. "Sometimes they want things to be gory . . . because it's gross and exciting."

He nods: of course people do.

Before the Druids-built-it theory took hold, Stonehenge's long-standing origin story involved Arthurian legend. Geoffrey of Monmouth, the twelfth-century Welsh historian, recounts in the colorful and quasi-factual *The History of the Kings of Britain* that Merlin had stolen the stones from Ireland, where they'd form a mountaintop circle in "Killaraus" and were valued for their "medicinal virtue." Using ingeniously devised "engines," Merlin helped the British transport the stones to their current site. But Geoffrey also notes that these stones originally came from *Africa*, whence the Irish had gotten them. This all sounds so nutty to modern ears we don't think twice about dismissing it.

But myths like these may transmit garbled truths within the fictions. What memories or desires could be buried in them?

Why, for one, does the story involve Ireland? Stonehenge's bluestones did indeed come from an equally and improbably faraway location, though from coastal Wales rather than an Irish mountain.

Why Merlin? Arthurian legend sites are so widespread in southwest England and Wales, it can seem comical: Merlin is buried in at least a dozen places. And many of these Arthurian places—in Wiltshire, Somerset, Devon, Cornwall—are located exactly where megalithic stone circles and passage tombs are found, including many "Excalibur stones" that were originally Neolithic standing stones. This striking overlap may suggest a root connection between these stories and prehistoric sites (including Merlin's own pre-Christian incarnation as a Celtic deity).

Finally, why Africa? It could just reflect a cultural desire to seem "worldly." But I will add that once, while in Tunisia visiting a museum exhibition on Carthage, I was startled to see a map of the Phoenician tin trading routes circa three thousand years ago—one that stretched all the way to southwest England. It seems Africa was not so distant from Britain in ancient times.

"Anything goes" is not the answer to Stonehenge's mysteries. But neither is discounting outright all the beliefs it has captured over the centuries, like a magnet collecting metals both common and rare. Five thousand years is a *very* long time for people to have paid attention to a single, human-created place, to have recreated its history, over and over, and with so many meanings.

9. Medium (7:10 a.m.)

Even just an hour at the Stone Circle has felt like an improvised performance of exploration and imagination. But now we're boarding the departing shuttle bus with all the other visitors— who will be featured in my photos of the place, somehow as prominently as the stones.

Soon my family will drive to Woodhenge, the remnants of a wooden-post version of Stonehenge about a mile northeast and dating to the Bronze Age. And there, further up the road, we will run across the largest archaeological dig in England's history: Durrington Walls, a long-buried Bronze Age village that housed the people who built Stonehenge's sarsen circle and trilithons. The site contains at least five hundred houses and evidence of massive barbecues that daily fed thousands of people. But this peak inhabitation only occurred over about a fifty-year span, starting around 2600 BCE—and, more interestingly, only during the winter season, centered around the December 21 solstice.

What the Durrington Walls site shows us is that those prehistoric builders and their families poured *everything* they had into Stonehenge's construction—vast quantities of livestock and grains, stonemasonry and woodworking skills, ingenious engineering and architectural planning, and precious good years of their own brief lives (people then rarely lived past age thirty). Since soft available metals such as copper, tin, and gold did them little good in construction, the technology they used was stone.

It can seem funny to call honed rock a technology—a word we now elide with digital apparatus and virtual media that swiftly collect and transmit unimaginable quantities of data. Our current technologies, in fact, stand as the symbolic opposites of stone: instead of rooting us to a single place or time, they grant us endless quick escapes to the near future, like always-waiting express trains out of the present moment and spot. And while they save us time in all manner of communication, commerce, and entertainment, they also dazzle our attention, flooding sugar-rushes of easy data that often eat away the time they'd saved us, and then some.

We like these technologies, or at least allow them to proliferate, because they mimic reality well enough, save for one crucial element: time flattens into an endless digital scrolling, a stamp on an email, text, or post, divested from any natural cycle. If it feels lifeless, it also seems deathless. All our digital bits and bobs—our logged-in keystrokes shedding like hair—are immortal in cyberspace.

But there's no avoiding this: Time is the medium through which we live. It's the messages we shape from it—our arts, cultures, technologies—that change the myths we create, the structures we devise, the beauties we observe about it.

"Technology" itself derives from the ancient Greek *tekno-logia*, meaning the communication or, literally, word (*logia*) of an art or craft (*tekno*). Which might explain why Stonehenge's "primitive" technology of stone still speaks to us and strikes so deeply, as if in a lost first tongue. No matter how "wired" we get, its art and craft remains immediate and eloquent.

Perhaps more than ever, Stonehenge manifests an architecture of sky and light, the motions of moon and sun, human bones and desire to be healed, mineral permanence and ephemeral season, a circle for song and gathering. Left to stand for 5,100 years, it's become a technology of human meaning, to be In Search Of: what becomes as time imprints our minds and bodies each moonrise and sunset and solstice, each illness and funeral and birth, each story and hope and theory about this singular transformative setting. Stonehenge holds it all in place, vast shards of our root genius: the ceaseless capacity for measuring, creating, and marvelous noticing.

MYSTERY HOUSE

> Architecture is how the person
> places herself in the space.
>
> —ZAHA HADID

1. Front Door

It's open. You enter the vast, rambling house, a curious architectural pastiche of midcentury American ranch and elegant
London Victorian, suburban Texan McMansion staircase and
Californian Spanish tile work, double-wide trailer screen doors
and New England saltbox attic, among myriad random features.

In this house you have seventeen bedrooms all to yourself.
The novelty of so many beds, so many closets filled with your
things leads you onward. But these bedrooms range across four
different continents, so you often wonder which country you
are in, which time zone. Their dwellings have fused into a single gangly and shifting structure, one ranging across time and
space, messing wildly with proportion and dimension. You
cross erratic parts of the world as you visit seventeen kitchens,
the seventeen rooms where your brother slept, your parents'
seventeen bedrooms.

You lived in seventeen homes growing up, but how you remember these places—how you experience them now—is as this whole yet mishmash structure. Counting all the floor plans reveals that you grew up in 134 rooms. So, a sort of mansion! A wandering, laws-of-physics-defying, decor-clashing mansion. A mansion lacking in clear boundaries, encompassing bits of Latin America and Alaska, Arabia and California, London and Houston, prefab and bespoke, gorgeous and hideous, common and bizarre. Uncounted corridors break off in all directions, to trick doors and staircases, abrupt entryways to eras and hemispheres, rerouting to forgotten wings, to nowhere, to your life now, to hundreds and hundreds of doorways.

You sometimes find yourself in this building without knowing how you got there. A wall will fall away and you're inside this collection of architectures that adheres yet shifts around, as if part liquid or seamed with foam. And you begin wandering its rooms again, searching for answers—as if, like a treasure hunt, you could find them if you looked hard enough.

2. Corridor

This memory palace of seventeen homes raises so many questions—tricky, regenerating, logistical ones. It was built, you often suspect, in order to ask them, a maze-like structure ever leading to more queries.

Why, for example, did your parents keep changing houses even after your family moved back to the States? During those years they bought places to remodel and sell at a profit. Each home became a financial springboard, an investment in a better "someday" to which the present tense could never catch up.

And from these renovation projects you learned the endlessly revisable, eerily delicate nature of housing, where the solid form of your shelter could suddenly give way to elemental components: The fine-boned wooden skeleton within each one. The chalky ceramic clatter of bathroom tile pried off with a chisel. The rough yet exacting jewelry collection of nails, screws, nibs. The holistic mess of renovation, like a precisely calculated bomb had gone off in your domestic world, its rubble and dust descended like a permanent, blanketing fixture. And then one day the mess disappeared like it had never been there, revealing order and calm in three inanimate dimensions.

Then it all started again, in a new house and its problem set of square footage, directional orientation, views or shadows, paint colors, door handles, metal faucet colors and finishes.

And then it all started again.

And again. And . . .

Were your parents building something extraordinary, beautiful, and useful, refashioning their world according to their own vision and creativity? Or were they trying to outrun or distract themselves from their various anxieties, unwanted pasts, ghosts? What degree of each impulse drove them—or drives you, or any of us, as we make and remake our lives?

3. Winchester

Near one of your family's homes loomed America's largest and most eccentrically designed "haunted" house, Sarah Winchester's mansion in San Jose, California, a state historical landmark where facts and legends compete for strangeness. Its commercial name is trademarked by the property's current owners—a name inspired by a 1924 visit by famed illusionist Harry Houdini, who dubbed it "a mystery." You will refer to it here as Sarah Winchester's house.

The legend goes like this: Mrs. Winchester, a wildly rich Victorian woman, moved from Connecticut to San Jose, bought a house, and then added onto it continuously for thirty-eight years. Her construction crews rebuilt and renovated it around-the-clock from 1884 until her death in 1922. Today the three-story Queen Anne mansion still stands, a 24,000-square-foot structure ranging across the 4.5-acre grounds. It contains 160 rooms, including 6 kitchens, 40 bedrooms, and 13 bathrooms—all built for use by its sole full-time occupant.

What drove this frenzy of construction? According to lore, Sarah Winchester suffered from a debilitating combination of grief, insanity, and inherited wealth.

Back in New Haven, Connecticut, Winchester's only child had died of a painful illness in infancy; then her husband died of tuberculosis in his prime. She would never again have a family of her own. But widowhood left Sarah Winchester one of the richest women in the world. Her husband had been sole heir to the vast Winchester gun fortune.

Driven mad by grief, as one completely unverified rumor goes, Winchester visited a medium. Through this medium, the ghost of Winchester's husband told her she must hide from the spirits of the dead killed by Winchester rifles—the uncountable multitudes of them, the Native American dead, the cowboy and pioneer dead—by building a house that is never completed. If the house is ever finished, the ghosts will find Sarah and murder her.

This tale explains why Sarah Winchester designed and oversaw the construction of her San Jose house for decades. And why she supposedly slept in a different bedroom each night, wearing a veil to disguise her identity. And why she had so many strange features built into the house—to confuse all those ghosts.

And it's true that several staircases lead into ceilings. One door opens to a two-story drop. Windows are built into floors. Lusciously hued Tiffany windows hang on a wall within a room that receives no natural light. Long staircases feature steps with only a two-inch rise. A so-called Seance Room on the top floor features spy holes and doors hidden behind wall panels. Secret passageways run beside corridors. Sarah's servants could get lost for hours if they took one wrong turn.

These are some legends and features visitors taking the thirty-six-dollar mansion tour learn about the popular tourist site.

4. Woodland

You were eleven when your family bought a home about three miles south of Sarah Winchester's house in the neighboring town of Campbell. Her village-sized mansion stood out in the suburban flatlands, shopping malls, and subdivisions of Silicon Valley like a lavish and anachronistic amusement park: some-place fanciful, Disneylandish, unreal.

But when your family toured Sarah Winchester's house, it felt half wild, like a painted woodland of architecture: brambles of high-ceilinged rooms and corridors shot off in all directions, clattering with visitors. The house smelled like every Bay Area Victorian in heat, the comforting chemical scent of oil-based dried paint, and beneath that a redwood forest's deep, feathery sweetness. Sarah Winchester's hand seemed everywhere in this mansion run amok out of a single mind, like a dream's endless house made material. Where the architectural features weren't bizarre or numbingly repetitive, they were strikingly beautiful: a ballroom of intimate dimensions, inlaid with polished multi-colored hardwoods in exquisite patterns, built with almost no nails, all to provide perfect acoustic conditions for Winchester's beloved chamber music performances.

One thing the place did not much resemble was a home, a space to be lived in by actual people. *Crazy rich lady* was what you tried to think of her, thanks to the tour and the tales it regurgitates and embellishes from a few old newspaper reports. These stories imply: what reason other than *insanity* could drive a woman to build such a large house over so many years?

Maybe the house embodied some kind of experiment, an obsessive inquiry into householdhood that repeated itself in every direction—in its forty-seven fireplaces, ten thousand window panes, two thousand doors. But what was the question? If Winchester was as unstable as those old legends claim, then the question may not matter; it may only reflect the fun-house distortions of grave mental illness. But did Winchester suffer from any such illness?

5. Plastic Windows

Your house about three miles south was the kind fairly described as "featureless," though features it had. A modest ranch on Coventry Drive, it stood in a circa-1950s tract in which Ye Olde English Cottage decorative elements were incorporated using cheap, ersatz materials: yellow plastic panels instead of glass in the dining room built-ins, fake wood paneling sheathing room after room in grainy plastic, maroon kitchen floor linoleum indented in brick-like shapes.

It was a house your mother hated with a passion you had never before seen directed at a building, a house your father dedicated himself to as a constant weekend chore. Together, your parents tore out all the faux English schmaltz, installed

hardwood floors, took the walls down to the studs and recon-
structed them with fresh wallboard, painted them light and
clean. Size-wise, it was just right for your family of four: With
three bedrooms, two bathrooms, and a living room that opened
onto the backyard, it had 153 fewer rooms than Sarah Winchester's house. Nobody could get lost in it.

But in some ways, your family was already lost. If all the
houses you lived in formed a maze, then the Campbell house
was seen by your parents as yet another dead-end. They couldn't
wait to sell it, move out of it, keep surging forward along a different path.

6. Maze

A maze is more complex—and more fun—than a labyrinth. It is
a puzzle-containing choice: You may pick multiple paths along
the way, series of corridors running in various directions, most
of which lead to dead-ends. By trial and error, by moving forward and backtracking along these nested, interlocking routes,
you can find the exit from the larger structure.

Of course, most children could tell you this. Your son drew
maze after maze for you to solve starting when he was about six
years old. As kids, we fully understand how the pleasure of getting lost is itself the process of discovery.

A labyrinth, on the other hand, is a tool for contemplation
and is just not as immediately entertaining. A single path leads
only to the center and back out again, without any detours or
false routes. Our interest in labyrinths rests with the visual
beauty and symbolic fateful journey of its design: walking the
classic labyrinth in Chartres Cathedral, for example, can represent the mind's movement toward the heart of perfect belief,
then back out again to the imperfect world. There is no false

path in this course. The believer, while walking, may contemplate the many interwoven circuits of her faith, the spiraling directions in which it may lead her. But the path itself is clear and singular.

A maze requires no faith at all. A maze is like a map depicting where we already live, how we tend to get through any given day, bumping against various sorts of walls, backtracking, getting stuck in a snarl of multiple possible trajectories. And what happens when we emerge at the exit? We usually look for another, more intricate maze to tackle.

7. Bridge

How does your mother stand at the stove in the prefab kitchen of your Colombian jungle house, boiling water so you can all drink it without getting sick, the iron-red mud and damp gold-green skies glowing from the window above the sink, and when you turn around you're gripping the banister at the top of the carved wooden staircase in your suburban Houston McMansion? You join your little brother on the thick beige carpeting in the high-ceilinged family room to watch TV sitcom reruns starring picturesquely average American families in quintessential American homes. Then you stand up and leap across a kind of fabric bridge—viscous, instantaneously sprung—to the glass-walled living room of your family's sprawling rented house in the Los Gatos hills, where your dad, alive and well, is reading the paper, as you admire the beautiful blue and white room your mother has designed there, the vast sparkle of Silicon Valley below you, and relax as if all this glistening finery was inherited, solid, and yours. Then you step backward six years, turn, and curl yourself on your twin bed in Dhahran, run your fingers over the rocks you have collected from the Eastern Arabian desert outside your door, clear clusters of spiky quartz crystal sharp as cat's teeth.

Your parents built this mansion of houses, even as they tore it down, religiously, with each move. But it lives on, rebuilding itself mysteriously, in you.

You are haunted by this house.

No, it's the opposite: *You* are what haunts this impossible home. You are the spirit, however faint, that still resides in each conjured room. You are the ghost wandering the halls, searching for answers—why your family lived this way, why not even beauty fused with safety was enough to make them stay, anywhere. Why your parents couldn't see all the ways *shelter* is a basic, profound necessity.

When we feel haunted by our memories, we really mean that we cannot stop haunting our own history. We've devised a maze into our pasts through which we may wander at will, bumping up against all the familiar old terrains and some forgotten ones.

You have never believed in ghosts, in spirits or souls wafting around a place to which they are tied. But a place can surely conjure our own memories—and there we may go, flying off, haunting our previous lives, eras, worlds.

8. Labyrinth

"Mrs. Winchester was as sane and clear headed a woman as I have ever known, and she had a better grasp of business and financial matters than most men. The commonly believed supposition that she had hallucinations is all bunk." This statement comes from Roy Leib, law partner and son of Frank Leib, Sarah Winchester's longtime attorney and friend, in a 1925 interview.

Her chauffeur, Fred Larsen, said in defense of Sarah Win-

chester against the rumor-mongers of her later years: "She
wasn't crazy. She was a plenty smart woman, and she had all
these people pegged as plain busybodies."

In a profile of Sarah Winchester in a 1911 issue of the *San
Jose News and Herald*, reporter Merle H. Gray stated unequivo-
cally that Winchester "is not a spiritualist . . . but is of an ortho-
dox faith." He also illuminated how she educated herself as an
architect and designer: "She read the best literature on this
subject to be obtained and was a subscriber to many technical
magazines in both English and French. . . . She builded slowly
and planned each staircase, window and wing in the establish-
ment. She considered the place her workshop and was such an
ardent devotee to her art that she had little time to make new
acquaintances."

These quotes are featured in the extensively researched
2010 biography of Sarah Winchester, *Captive of the Labyrinth*, in which historian, professor, and author Mary Jo Ignoffo
redresses many legends and false rumors concerning Winchester using primary sources, letters, interviews, and other
factual evidence.

9. Perimeter

Your first house growing up was a colonial-style saltbox in Burlington, Vermont; your last house was a classic California ranch,
crisply hand-painted gray with white trim by your parents, in
San Anselmo, California. Each home an emblem of American
suburban architecture. And Burlington and San Anselmo: these
are fortunate, beautiful places to claim as one's own.

So that's two homes of the seventeen. Here's the rest, in a
jumble as always. You lived in a double-wide trailer near the Arabian Gulf and a Los Gatos hills view house, a trailer miles out-

side Fairbanks, Alaska, and a wood-clad townhouse in downtown Houston. Your family's stick-built three-bedroom in the sands of Dhahran, Saudi Arabia, resembled your stucco ranchita in the San Francisco Bay Area hillside tract of Almaden. You called an expensive furnished flat near London's Kensington Square Garden home, as well as a sprawling suburban Tudor-style two-story in The Woodlands, Texas. You lived in a single-wide trailer in a Colombian jungle, then in a nearby kit-built bungalow infested with albino tree frogs. You moved to three different houses in Marin County, California, alternating hillside locations with the flats: beside the San Anselmo ranch, these include a hillside Terra Linda 1960s midcentury one-story and a 1930s terra cotta–colored Mediterranean near downtown San Anselmo. You lived in a low-rise apartment building on a busy street in San Jose, California; and your grandparents' sprawling duplex with the walled rose garden, also in San Jose; and the ranch near Sarah Winchester's house in Campbell.

Each home forms a bit of time that wraps through you, tied like a colored ribbon to a particular grouping of months, and, at the longest span of time, three years.

10. Flow

You could alphabetize the seventeen homes by country, then city. Or you could organize them by your favorite room in descending order. You could enumerate them by square footage, smallest to largest.

You could list them by year, assigned to your age, broken down by month: the staid, sensible, and—to you—mind-numbing sequence of linear narrative, nearly all biographies. Except you never remember the homes in chronological order. This makes some sense. We don't live in a house chronologically, after all.

We live in houses spatially, viscerally, in a way that snares and nets time into blocks of identifiable life and emotional imprints. This is what fascinates about architecture: an art form unfolding in three dimensions, or, adding in our experience of place through time, four. Add in memory or daydreams, five—or, depending on the person, some exponential factor.

And what if the sequence that unfolds, the simple progressive clockwork of hours, weeks, years, does little to explain the real meaning? Your brother's snug, pale yellow and white London bedroom where he and you hung out for hours every day in the window seat, reading and drawing, dissolves without warning to the sunny farmhouse kitchen in San Anselmo a decade later, one wall hung with shiny copper pans, where your mom is marinating flank steak with lime juice and garlic and salt, your dad just outside the open sliding door on the patio tending the barbecue. These are favorite rooms, casually lovely arrangements of your family.

Your mother always talked about the "flow" of a floor plan: How logical is the layout? How well does one room lead, comfortably and even graciously, to the next? These were ideas you were raised to understand the importance of, while also, somewhat ironically, rarely experiencing in the larger structure of your young life. In this memory palace of houses, the maze of them, you gravitate to the flourishing scenes, the bright and charming rooms, the just-missed parallel universes that open onto this question: "What would have happened had we stayed here?" Then the brightness fades and you're in a hall of locked doors, where you stand, twisting the handles.

11. Relativity

"Relativity" is one of M. C. Escher's most famous prints—copies have hung in college dorm rooms since it first appeared in 1953. It depicts a single building possessing three distinct orientations of gravity, three simultaneous, impossible, yet geometrically interconnected horizon lines. What this *looks* like are rooms, hallways, staircases, and windows fused seamlessly at space-bending twists, around which faceless mannequin-like figures stroll. The floor under the feet of one walking figure appears as a wall for another, as perspective shifts throughout the structure at ninety-degree angles, and seemingly in three dimensions. Among other things, it provides a supreme exercise in *disorientation*. And you've always wondered: is it a scene that visualizes memories lived by the same person overlaid across a single place?

Your mystery house often feels like this. It curves around constantly, revealing a deep hall closet where you used to hide under blankets with a book and flashlight; the summer sunlight streaming across your white-and-violet bedspread in Alaska. All such places are manifold and inviolate, as much as the remembered figures set to wander them.

Or are they? Is memory itself a form of design, a renovation of the past? It does seem to burrow its own dimensions, rerouting space and time by the quantum mechanics of logic and emotion, impulse and desire. It holograms the essence of our own experiences as they have grown inside us, shape-shifted with meaning, vital and precise as life forms.

12. Library

Here are some remarkable features of Sarah Winchester's house—all elements she designed herself:

Sarah Winchester's house was the first in California to feature gas-fueled heat. Her house-wide gas lighting system was then the largest in the state.

Her home was one of the earliest in the state to contain fully plumbed bathrooms. And it was the first in California to possess hot-water showers.

She designed and had installed a very early example of an intercom system so that she and her staff could converse across the house's great span.

Most remarkably, Sarah Winchester's house featured an extensive and intricate water catchment system, one that funnels rainwater through wall-embedded grilles and pipes into cisterns to be used during dry months for the extensive gardens and grounds. This system would be considered innovative and effective even in California today—when, despite the state's many droughts, such sophisticated water recycling features are still the rare exception in residential or commercial buildings.

Sarah Winchester served as both architect and engineer of these projects, self-educating herself in both roles. She amassed a vast library of hundreds of books, technical manuals, and current periodicals on architecture and architectural engineering published in both English and French (in which she was fluent). Her library of French literature alone was considered the largest such collection on the West Coast.

13. Louis Kahn

Louis Kahn asked one of the strangest and most useful questions of architectural design: "What does a brick want to be?" He asked it as an architect, envisioning how a material shapes both the site and the conceptual style of a building's structure. But we can ask a similar question of any structure, even long after it is built: What does a *house* want to be? It helps us to understand our own worlds, particularly the ones we did not choose, growing up.

Sometimes a house wants to be your mother. Sometimes a house wants to hide the evidence. Some houses would smother you with good tastefulness, a claustrophobic need to impress. Some houses would like you to calm down already. Some houses want you to get the hell out. Some houses get silly with nostalgia. Some houses are destined for the aftermaths of true love. Some houses couldn't care less: you might as well be living in generic anywhere. But no one ever is. By trying so hard to say nothing, the house is saying, "This box is all you get."

Your mother always knew exactly what your homes wanted to be. She pored over design magazines, clipping her favorite photos from *Architectural Design* and *House & Garden*, collecting swatches of paint and fabric, many of which came with you on your moves. Your travels to two dozen countries often involved her pointing out the medieval wooden beams, the Islamic tile work, the Norman arches, the Art Nouveau banisters, but also, equally, the unpleasant green paint in the restaurant, the classic black stripe on the hotel drapes, the porcelain vases cleverly transformed into table lamps.

Your mother used her laser-fine eye for design to "do up" each house far above par and always on the fly. In coastal Jubail, Saudi Arabia, in 1979, in a compound of at least a hundred identical trailers, your double-wide won a "best designed" award in a Ladies Auxiliary Club competition thanks to your mom's decorating prowess. As a grade-schooler, you could not have been prouder to live in such a pretty trailer.

And so you assumed early on that each of your homes was, at root, an environmental manifestation of your mother.

14. Earthquake

Some reasonable theories explain why Sarah Winchester built her extraordinary house the way she did, and why it looks like it does today. (These theories are meticulously researched and outlined in historian Ignoffo's biography of Winchester.)

Sarah Winchester suffered from a severe, disfiguring case of rheumatoid arthritis, which is why she wore a veil over her face. And it's this debilitating arthritis that explains the long staircases with the two-inch step rises: they made her walks from one story to the next much less painful, and even possible.

As for the house's glaringly strange features—the trick doors and dangerous drops, the staircases that slam into walls—there is this fact: none of these elements existed before April 18, 1906. On that day, the house, along with much of the Bay Area, was ravaged by the San Francisco earthquake centered along the San Andreas Fault that registered a catastrophic 8.0 on the Richter scale.

Afterward, Sarah Winchester evaluated the widespread damage to her house—including the toppled tower, whose seven stories had been felled to three—and chose to cut her losses. Instead of a full restoration, she made the hardheaded decision to not pour any more serious money into her mansion. She directed her builders to perform what was essentially emergency surgery on many collapsed rooms, wings, and floors. And so several staircases were boarded up; holes in the walls were sheathed with new walls. Structural integrity took precedence over architectural elegance.

Today the mansion looks like it was designed, in part, without any order in mind. But it is, in fact, a building only partially renovated after surviving a devastating natural disaster. Mrs. Winchester moved to a houseboat during the basic fixes, and when she returned to live at her San Jose mansion full time, she made herself at home in one small part of it: a wing that somewhat miraculously remained in perfect condition.

15. Setting

Where the family takes place, its natural setting, is one form of home or other.

And your own mystery house, growing up, turned "home" into a verb—trickily and continuously conjugating itself into present, past, past perfect, and past continuous tenses. In the sheer amount of activity it required, "home" for you and your family was always a quest.

But where was the quest leading? What was its purpose, its object?

Often, your parents aimed your family toward a mythical destination: the Someday House, the One True Home. It performed a tantalizing legend, a parallel track of history that ran alongside the actual one, like a secret corridor waiting to be discovered and lead you all to your rightful lives. If you could only find it, then you could settle down.

But isn't this how we all feel at times? That some destiny has eluded us. The degree to which it has, and the importance or beauty of that destiny, and even how many destinies are in play, are a few of the twinges we may feel. For your parents, the pressure to discover this perfect home seemed real, exhausting, and quixotic.

To write about a home is to write, eventually, about its destruction. "You can't go home again" is this effect in its simplest, least rubble-producing form. And is this why taking a sledgehammer to the walls is one of life's most satisfying pleasures?

You sometimes step into your old house in San Anselmo, the gray and white ranch with the backyard trellis wound with grapevines, and wonder—very simply—why your parents couldn't have stayed there. Be happy with what you have: Isn't this the clarion call of the American loser? Who are you to ask someone else to settle, to take up less space than they want, feel they deserve to? But of course this is not what you are asking.

To settle, or to settle down: for you, these are antonyms. The first means an acceptance of failure, the second a hope for success. In your mind, your mystery house, they lead in two different directions: one into a maze and the other forming a labyrinth, a pathway to its symbolic peaceful core.

16. Medium

As an eleven-year-old visiting Sarah Winchester's house, you wanted to believe it was haunted. But even at that age, you could not convince yourself of any such nonsense. You stood in her last bedroom, in the wing she'd retired to after the 1906 earthquake and where she lived until her death in 1922, at age eighty-two—a room that should, of any spot in the mansion, be "haunted." Yet you noticed how normal it was, how calm and restful. You remember your dad commenting on that, too—saying something like, "nice room"—and you nodded and watched your mother inspect the carved wooden dresser. Sunlight streamed across the high, old-fashioned bed, the kind that look so stiff and uncomfortable now but was conventional in Victorian times. The intimate, private, humble room humanized Sarah Winchester, even with all the visitors stomping through it looking for the bizarre, the grotesque, ephemeral signs of an eternally miserable soul wafting around. But there was no whiff of doom or horror. Winchester built her house until she lost interest in designing it any further, then retired to a comfortable corner of the domestic universe she'd created.

Some people need to build things. Is this the simple and truthful explanation for Sarah Winchester's life and house? Some people are driven to make; it is in the doing that they live. What's rare is that Sarah Winchester was wildly rich; was free of the responsibilities of husband and children in an era when family ruled, and exclusively, women's lives; and was passionately fascinated by architecture at a time when women were never trained for skilled professions, never mind as architects. If she'd been a man of similar passions and means and willpower, who would have questioned her desire to make for its own sake, to learn and grow through the design and construction of an inanimate, three-dimensional medium that takes up one hell of a lot of space? In any built-up place, that's what men do and have done for centuries, for millennia. How could a woman want to do this? Well, the mystery might really be: Why haven't more?

17. Artist

Your mother tells you this now: she would do it all over again, exactly the same way. Every move had an excellent reason at the time, a logical progression from one home directly to the next.

You can't see the larger structure they created as seamless, functional architecture. But she can.

She muses about her old houses as if she'd just stopped by them yesterday. "You should have seen the wallpaper in Almaden," she says, and describes, in minute detail, the blue paisley-printed wallpaper she'd used in the en suite bathroom in 1973. Or the cream wallpaper dotted with pale yellow roses she put up in your bedroom in The Woodlands, Texas, the paper you'd proudly picked out with her at the special wallpaper store. Or in your snug second-story nursery in Burlington, Vermont—in a house you don't remember but feel as if you do—there is more wallpaper: robin's egg blue with tiny pink and yellow flecks. Wallpaper is one key element beloved only by the artists, the rare and gifted people, whose medium is houses.

It's an expensive art form, houses.

You turn to look at it again, from here. It still appears as a maze, ungainly and worryingly large. It may not ever make sense to you. It surely is not practical. It may be, in some ways, foolish or tragic. But it is extraordinary. You were raised in place with, if not two thousand doors, then something close: someone else's dream home that fit otherness and familiarity, safety and journey under one roof.

SELECTED SOURCES

I began writing memoir essays in 2015 with one overarching goal: to create narratives that connect my personal experiences to the larger world, specifically those byways, parts of town, and bookstore sections that fascinate me the most. Out of the "research" known as "years passing"—and the attendant reading for pleasure, watching of movies, listening to music, wandering through museums, and sometimes revisiting old neighborhoods—these pieces started to cohere in my notebooks.

For "A History of Nomadism," I reread my copies of Gaston Bachelard's *The Poetics of Space* (Boston: Beacon Press, 1994), Bruce Chatwin's *The Songlines* (New York: Penguin Books, 1987), Isabelle Eberhardt's *The Oblivion Seekers* (San Francisco: City Lights, 1975), T. E. Lawrence's *Seven Pillars of Wisdom* (New York: Anchor Books/Doubleday, 1991), Wilfred Thesiger's *Arabian Sands* (London: Penguin Books, 2007), and the article edited by my great-uncle Gilbert Drake Harlan, "The Diary of Wilson Barber Harlan: A Walk with a Wagon Train" (*Journal of the West* 3, no. 2 [April 1964]). I sought out Yi-Fu Tuan's *Space and Place: The Perspective of Experience* (Minneapolis: University of Minnesota Press, 2014), Jibrail S. Jabbur's *The Bedouins and the Desert: Aspects of Nomadic Life in the Arabic East* (Albany: State University of New York Press, 1995), and Marcel Kurpershoek's *Arabia of the Bedouins* (London: Saqi Books, 2001). And I stumbled on a treasure trove of nomadic history and its how-to logistical realities in Torvald Faegre's *Tents: Architecture of the Nomads* (New York: Anchor Books, 1979)—an out-of-print, hand-illustrated guide that helped me understand the shared, worldwide human heritage of woven, moveable architecture.

For "Spider Season," I consulted (often with a hand over my eyes) Richard Bradley's *Common Spiders of North America* (Berkeley: University of California Press, 2012), and pored over Leonardo da Vinci's *Notebooks: Oxford World's Classics* (Oxford: Oxford University Press, 2008). For "Motel Childhood," I pulled down my old copy of L. Frank Baum's *Ozma of Oz* (New York: Rand McNally, 1907) from my son's bookshelf and checked out an entertaining cultural history, *The Motel in America*, by John A. Jakle, Keith A. Sculle, and Jefferson S. Rogers (Baltimore: Johns Hopkins University Press, 1996).

For "Several Londons, 1977," I attempted to time-travel to 1977 London by first getting my hands on Berlitz Guides' staff-written 1977 guidebook *London* (worth it for the street shots alone). I already had Guy Debord's *The Society of the Spectacle* (Detroit: Black and Red, 1983), thanks to a heady Marxist theory section of a philosophy class back in college. I read John Lydon's riveting and often hilarious autobiography, *Rotten: No Irish, No Blacks, No Dogs* (New York: Picador, 1994), in which he allows friends, enemies, and even journalists to add in their own voices, *Rashomon*-style, to his version of events. Jon Savage's *England's Dreaming: Anarchy, Sex Pistols, Punk Rock, and Beyond* (New York: St. Martin's Griffin, 2001) is doubtless the most lyrical book ever written on punk. And I watched and rewatched Julien Temple's brilliant documentary, *The Filth and the Fury: A Sex Pistols Film* (Fine Line Features, 2000).

For "Mobile Home," I found inspiration (and some good puns) in Allan D. Wallis's *Wheel Estate: The Rise and Decline of Mobile Homes* (Oxford: Oxford University Press, 1991) and again revisited L. Frank Baum's work, this time *The Wizard of Oz* (New York: Rand McNally, 1900).

For "Likelers," I drew from Paul Adamson's beautiful, weighty *Eichler: Modernism Rebuilds the American Dream* (Salt Lake City: Gibbs Smith, 2002) for some details about Joseph Eichler's biography and Eichler history. That led me to several books by Frank Lloyd Wright, including *An Organic Architecture: The Architecture of Democracy* (Cambridge, MA: MIT Press, 1970). And I revisited the story of Steve Jobs's childhood home via Luke Dormehl's "How a California Real Estate Developer Helped Create Apple as We Know It" (*Cult of Mac* [blog], March 15, 2015).

For "Dadaholic," I perused my dad's original copy of Barbara B. Brown's *New Mind, New Body: Bio-feedback, New Directions for the Mind* (New York: Bantam Books, 1979). I am very grateful to have found Gabor Maté's *In the Realm of Hungry Ghosts* (Berkeley: North Atlantic, 2010)—a standout on the subject of addiction. I confirmed the provenance of "Hey Jude" via Justin Wm. Moyer's article in the *Washington Post*, "How Cynthia Lennon's Doomed Marriage to John Lennon Inspired 'Hey Jude'" (April 2, 2015).

Archaeology has been a lifelong passion, and my research into "What Is Vanishing" started years ago with Rebecca Yamin's article "New York's Mythic Slum: Digging Lower Manhattan's Infamous Five Points" (*Archaeology* 50, no. 2 [March/April 1997]: 44–53). From there I discovered Anne-Marie Cantrell and Diana diZerega Wall's *Unearthing Gotham: The Archaeology of New York City* (New Haven: Yale University Press, 2001). On my visit to the African Burial Ground Monument, I picked up Martia G. Goodson's *New York's African Burial Ground* (a booklet published by Eastern National in 2012) and Joyce Hansen and Gary McGowan's *Breaking Ground, Breaking Silence: The Story of New York's African Burial Ground* (New York: Henry Holt, 1998). I consulted *Roads of Arabia: The Archaeological Treasures of Saudi Arabia*, edited by Ute Franke and Joachim Gierlichs (Tübingen, Germany: Ernst Wasmuth Verlag, 2012) for photos of and details on the Arabian artifacts featured in the museum exhibition by the same name.

"Setting Stonehenge" takes place over an hour but took weeks to research. I got Julian Richards's *Stonehenge* (London: English Heritage Guidebooks, 2015)—invaluable for its maps and diagrams—during my visit to the site. I dove into the key contemporary theories via Mike Parker Pearson's *Stonehenge: A New Understanding* (New York: The Experiment, 2013) and Timothy Darvill *Stonehenge: The Biography of a Landscape* (Gloucestershire: Tempus, 2006). I sourced old quotes on the stones from Ralph Waldo Emerson's *The Complete Works* (Boston and New York: Houghton Mifflin, 1904) and *Thomas Hardy: Interviews and Recollections*, edited by James Gilson (London: MacMillan, 1999). Twentieth-century Stonehenge was distinctively captured in Gerald S. Hawkins's *Stonehenge Decoded* (New York: Doubleday, 1965) and Alexander Thom's *Megalithic Sites in Britain* (Oxford: Oxford University Press, 1967). Nicholas Wade's "Celtic Found to Have Ancient Roots" (*New York Times*, July 1, 2003) and Colin Schultz's "Stone-